I've lost my little Willie!

A celebration of comic postcards

by Benny Green

ElmTree Books

For Betty

First published in Great Britain 1976
by Elm Tree Books Ltd
90 Great Russell Street, London WC1
and Arrow Books Ltd
3 Fitzroy Square, London W1

Text copyright © 1976 Benny Green
Postcards copyright © 1976 Bamforth Company
(Marketing) Ltd

Designed by Bernard Higton/Clift Jones Associates

The publishers gratefully acknowledge the cooperation
of Bamforth Company (Marketing) Ltd

Printed in Great Britain by
REDWOOD BURN LIMITED

SBN 241 89407 7

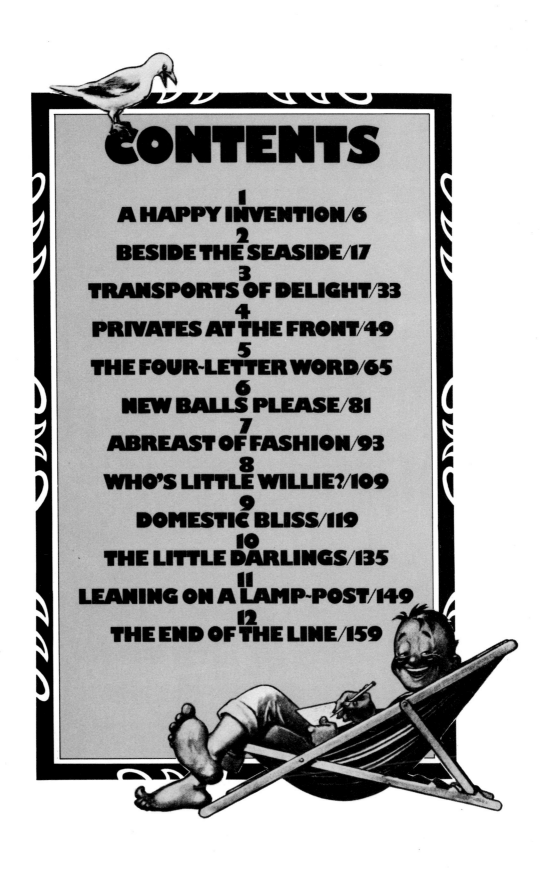

CONTENTS

1
A HAPPY INVENTION

In the year 1869 the Austrian Government, in a freakish and very nearly unique outburst of inventive resource, introduced a new method of communication called the Postal Card. This novel amenity was an economical and convenient arrangement by which you received through the post short messages from people with neither the inclination nor the intellectual power to send you any long messages. So far as the Austrians were concerned, the new Postal Card had only two drawbacks. First, the person delivering the card was at liberty to read its contents. In fact this danger was not as acute as it might appear, as very few of the postmen, or indeed anybody else in the Austro-Hungarian Empire, were able to read much. The other flaw was much more serious; in order to post one of the newfangled cards, you were obliged to affix to it a portrait of the Emperor Franz Josef. It speaks volumes for the attractiveness of the cards that not even the hideous facial aspect of the Austrian ruler could deter the population from proceeding with a positive orgy of postal-card exchange. In their first month the new cards reached sales of one and a half million.

The British, who at that time were interested in absolutely anything which sold a million and a half in a month, were not slow to follow the Habsburg lead. One year later the Rev. Francis Kilvert confided to his diary:

Sunday, October morrow: At the Vicarage I saw one of the first 'Post Cards' that have been sent. It was from Lilian to Mrs. Venables, very bright and cheery.

Tuesday, 4 October: Today I sent my first postcards, to my Mother, Thersie, Emmie and Perch. They are capital things, simple, useful and handy. A happy invention.

Kilvert's observations are of acute interest to all social

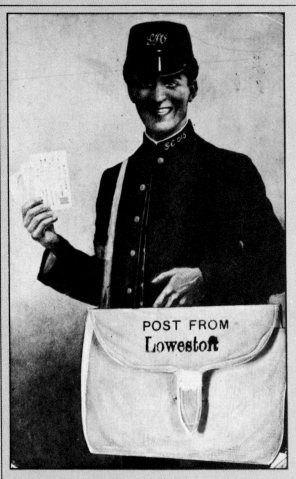

POST FROM
Lowestoft

with his chief offers an interesting glimpse of the kind of social climate in which the emergent art of the postcard began to flourish.

On first entering the postal service, young Trollope had made the alarming discovery that the only qualification required was idiocy:

I got into my place without any examining. Looking back now, I think I can see with accuracy what was then the condition of my own mind and intelligence. Of things to be learned by lessons I knew almost less than could be supposed possible after the amount of schooling I had received. I could read neither French, Latin, nor Greek. I could speak no foreign language. Of the merest rudiments of the sciences I was completely ignorant. My handwriting was in truth wretched. My spelling was imperfect. There was no subject as to which examination would have been possible on which I could have gone through an examination otherwise than disgracefully.

Clearly, Trollope was a model Post Office employee, and it is not surprising that, possessing as he did such a distinct intellectual advantage over his fellow-workers, he advanced so far up the Civil Service scale. Hill was his *bête noire*, of whom he later wrote, 'I believe him to be entirely unfit to manage men or arrange labour'. This indictment loses something of its effect when we learn that Trollope's own idea of how to manage men and arrange labour was to burst into a conference and shout, 'I differ from you entirely. What did you say?', an exhibition of unconscious buffoonery made even more hilarious by the fact that like a great many Victorians, Trollope sported the kind of beard which gives a man the look of someone who has just swallowed a horse and managed to get everything down except the tail. To all this Hill would peer coldly with his reptilian eyes through gold pince-nez, rather as though the creator

Sir Rowland Hill

historians, especially as the reverend gentleman seems to have been using a diary which left out the first two days of October. However, a more confident grasp of datelines can be found in the first mention of Postal Cards in *The Times*. The edition of 10 January 1871 reproduced the following item from the *Carlsruhe Gazette*:

POSTAL CARDS: Corresponding cards are visibly extending. Besides Germany and Austria-Hungary, where they originated, they have already been introduced into Denmark, France, Great Britain, Holland, Portugal, Roumania, Sweden, Switzerland, Spain and the United States. They are about to be adopted in Belgium and Italy.

We may well wonder what kept the British so long. After all, it was now more than thirty years since Sir Rowland Hill had revolutionised the whole concept of postal services with his Penny Post. Hill (1795–1879) had introduced the new cheap service with the aim of increasing Post Office revenues, and as the scheme was a sensible one, the Post Office naturally opposed it bitterly. But Hill had his way – which is about all he did have, for in the years since he has had a very bad press indeed, owing to his inconsiderate treatment of an obscure subordinate who resigned in a fit of pique one day after being passed over for promotion. Usually this type of storm in a bureaucratic teacup goes unnoticed by history, but unluckily for Hill the obscure subordinate turned out to be Anthony Trollope, who spent the rest of his life telling the world how odious Hill was, and whose feud

The Post Office's first postcard, issued in 1870

of Barsetshire were something which had just crawled out of an apple. And just to prove his loyalty to Hill, Trollope recollected, 'It was a pleasure to me to differ from him on all measures'.

Yet between them, this ill-assorted pair provided the two vital artefacts for the dissemination of the postcard. After you had purchased your card and composed your message, you performed two last actions. First you stuck on to your card one of Hill's stamps, and then you dropped your message into one of the pillar-boxes which Trollope had invented and which were placed at strategic points all over the four kingdoms. The stamp and the pillar-box; it is difficult to imagine two more influential factors in the burgeoning of social life in the nineteenth and early twentieth centuries. There was, however, a third, and it is characteristic of Hill's political generation that this third factor was not seriously considered when the Penny Post was first introduced. Hill had dreamed of coaxing revenue out of the *hoi polloi* by tempting them to send each other postal messages. Unfortunately, there was a snag. The *hoi polloi* could not read or write. A small thing perhaps, but enough to throw a spanner into the ambitious works of Hill who, like many a Victorian reformer, had locked the door before the horse had had a chance to get into the stable. The real golden age of epistolary Britain began with neither Hill's stamps nor Trollope's pillar-boxes, but with a significant parliamentary measure.

Let us advance our narrative by examining the observation of Sir Arthur Bryant: *The Penny Post, introduced by Rowland Hill in 1840, had led to a far-reaching change in social habit: in three years the weekly delivery of letters in the United Kingdom rose from a million and a half to nearly four million. Correspondence, hitherto an activity of the well-to-do classes alone, became common to all who could read or write.*

But what about those who couldn't read or write? The statistic of nearly four million missives a week sounds impressive until we remember that roughly three million of these appear to have been written by Queen Victoria to her relations. A more perceptive conclusion is drawn by W. J. Reader in his *Victorian England* when he says:

With the penny post the advantages and possibilities of town life became better and better known in the country. Booth, writing late in the century, considered that 'one of the most powerful and efficient migration agencies is the letters written home by the country girl settled in domestic service in the great town'. That of course, was after the Education Act of 1870 had added widespread literacy to the cheapness of the postal services, thus greatly increasing the number of potential letter writers. The vicar of East Dereham in Norfolk recorded in his diary that the number of letters passing through the local post office rose from 7,000 a week in 1873 to 25,000 a week in 1876.

One would have thought that the equation was irresistible. More literacy equals more reading and writing. But Victorian vicars had an amazing knack of concentrating on the right actions and then ascribing to them the wrong motives. Our vicar from East Dereham puzzled for a while over this spectacular rise in postal communications and then, bringing the mighty engines of a classical education to bear on the problem, finally announced that the increase in letters was due to the increase in population. Our first instinct is to rush to East Dereham, disinter all its later Victorian corpses and hope to discover the substance of the potent aphrodisiac which caused the birth rate to rise by nearly 400 per cent in three years. But Mr Reader's quiet tact functions as a useful corrective when he adds, 'The new schools may also have had something to do with it'.

As the germ of the Postal Card idea shuttled back

1890 card and envelope commemorating Penny Post

and forth between Austria-Hungary and Britain, and as it swiftly gained a hold across the rest of Europe, two new refinements were soon added, one legislative, the other commercial. At Berne, on 9 October 1874, the International Postal Convention regularised the process by which nations guaranteed delivery. And in Paris fifteen years later, at the Exhibition, some nameless hustler first thought of the idea of linking a card to a specific occasion and/or place. Visitors to the Paris Exhibition found themselves invited to buy a postcard of the Eiffel Tower at the Eiffel Tower, write it, and then post it *from* the Eiffel Tower, invariably composing their message as follows: 'This is where I am now'. This piece of monumentally pointless information was amended by a more sophisticated age to read: 'Having a wonderful time; wish you were here', a statement which was itself stood on its head in time by the wiseacres of Tin Pan Alley with 'Having a wonderful wish; time you were here'. The entrepreneurs of the Paris Exhibition set a pattern for others to follow, and for once the G.P.O. moved swiftly by duplicating the Paris ploy only a year later. At the Royal Naval Exhibition in 1890 you could buy a postcard depicting the Eddystone lighthouse, write your message and then post it from, of all things, the top of a model of the Eddystone lighthouse. But it was a further four years before the private printing of such cards became legal in Britain. The reason for this delay in granting the sanction of legality to so harmless a pursuit was simply that the panjandrums of State wanted to be quite sure that the manufacture of cards would not immediately result in the decline and fall of the British Empire.

But it is the final act of concession, in 1902, which is the most puzzling of all, because it appears to have acknowledged as legal the writing of messages on the address side of the card. The implication here is irresistible, that before the government passed this amendment, everybody had been sending blank cards to one another. Whatever the truth of the matter, it is from the moment of the 1902 legislation that statistics regarding the British postcard begin to become reliable.

The reader will probably have realised by now an irritating truth about postcard history, which is that in attempting to assess the speed and extent of their rise in popularity he is hampered by a deliberate confusion on the part of social historians between all post and letter post. When that vicar from East Dereham spoke of 25,000 items a week, clearly he meant letters *and* postcards; at first nobody bothered to differentiate between the two, and ever since then, a certain neglect of the postcard has remained apparent in the popular art of the West. It would somehow have been slightly absurd for Edgar Allan Poe to have composed a sinister short story called 'The Purloined Postcard', and the respectful attention of posterity would surely be distracted by a publication called, say, 'The Life, Letters and Postcards of William Ewart Gladstone'. Not even Thomas 'Fats' Waller, the last person in the world to bother with protocol, would have dreamed of recording a musical item with the title of 'I'm Gonna Sit Right Down and Write

The 1889 Paris Exhibition produced the first souvenir postcard

Myself a Postcard'. And yet it is arguable that the common or garden postcard, for all the exposed nature of its contents, has carried messages at least as pregnant as those which hide inside envelopes.

In 1903 the editor of a London newspaper prophesied that 'in ten years Europe will be buried beneath picture postcards'. Collecting became all the rage, and when the publishing house of Raphael Tuck offered a prize for the largest national collection of Tuck cards, the winner produced over 20,000. By 1908 the ancient dream of Sir Rowland Hill had come true. In Britain 860,000,000 cards were being sent and delivered annually, while in Germany, not far from the postcard's birthplace, the figure was twice as high.

So far as the home market was concerned, the Edwardian years, when legislation and technical experience had combined to remove the last impediments to the progress of the postcard, constitute a kind of golden age. Up to 1894 almost all the printing of British view-cards had been done in Germany; after the 1902 legislation local firms began to dominate, with the most spectacular results. One London Edwardian publisher estimated his postcard output at 50,000 a day, and the new firm of Wrench and Ettlinger took only three years to create a business with more than 5000 retail firms on its list and a monthly revenue from postcard sales of £4000. How had gentlemen like Wrench and Ettlinger stumbled

into this strange new industry? No doubt by pure accident, for there were no precedents, no training procedures, no statute of limitations in a branch of publishing which had only just begun to exist.

At which point we find ourselves confronted by an earnest mid-Victorian called James Bamforth. He lived in Holmfirth, last outpost on the Yorkshire side of the Pennines, one of those townships whose archetype appears in so many of the novels of J. B. Priestley, with their formidable choirs, their dark satanic mills and their even darker and even more satanic chapels, their cloth and their lowering, porous skies. Bamforth was the son of a painter and decorator and was no doubt expected to follow the same trade, a form of primogeniture mysteriously described by the Victorians as private enterprise. But Bamforth's was the generation which suddenly and most delightfully found itself floating on the buoyant waters of expectation inspired by the spirit of invention. It was photography which tempted Bamforth away from the family tradition, and in 1870, at just about the time when the harassed subjects of Franz Josef were pausing in their consumption of wiener schnitzel and goulash long enough to send each other Postal Cards about the Franco-Prussian War, he went into business for himself, manufacturing slides for the new-fangled Magic Lantern.

Bamforth was a thoughtful and conscientious man, and the quality of his work was high, largely due to his shrewd concentration on photographic plates rather than transparencies. Before long he had become the darling of the Temperance Societies and the Bands of Hope, travelling all over Yorkshire to deliver the crude message of charades like 'Slaves of Drink' to audiences whose idea of a bacchanalian orgy was the consumption of two successive mugs of cocoa. Often there was a musical accompaniment to these quaint recitals, from some wheezing grampus of a harmonium, and it is the effect of this musical element on Bamforth's subsequent career which illustrates the fortuitous nature of his progress as an entrepreneur. The musical accompaniment led to the production of a series of slides to illustrate popular songs and ballads, which in turn caused Bamforth to go into partnership with a Bradford firm for the production of what might loosely be described as moving pictures. Bamforth's first son Frank was the

director, his second son Edwin a bit-player, his third son Harry the distributor, his daughter Janie the continuity girl. (The convention had been established years before of augmenting the family talent with actresses and actors from local theatres.) By 1913 the production of short comedy films was Bamforth's main business concern, but the slides continued to flourish. Bamforth's proud boast was that any song on the market could be illustrated within the hour; his annual output was 600 new titles, the company stock numbered over 2,000,000 slides, and the 1905 catalogue contained 336 pages, including a 23-page index.

By this time the English had already begun to carry close to their hearts the postcard portraits of the various fluttery-eyed, wasp-waisted heroines of theatrical dreamland. It is not so easy for the disenchanted student of the 1970s to imagine how large these postcards might bulk in the lives of those who purchased them. But in a world where there was no radio or television, no fan clubs and almost no illustrated magazines with a mass circulation, no cinemas and almost no practical photography, how else was a romantically inclined young man to retain on the retina of his mind's eye the image of his dream-goddess? One day in 1902 the illegitimate son of an itinerant violinist managed to get a job in a Manchester theatre selling chocolates, a double stroke of prodigious good fortune, for not only did the boy need the money, but he also adored the theatre. The show was *Cinderella*, the chocolate-seller Neville Cardus, and every day for three months he studied the principals to the point where their impersonations were more real to him than the life outside in the streets. But the time came when the run of *Cinderella* ended, and the chocolate-seller was desolate:

Pain which I could not define came into my heart and stomach when I wondered where at this very minute all the scattered glories might chance to be. The dispersion of forces brought together, God knows how, for a moment – no, I was not sophisticated enough to understand the ironic flavour in my boyish sense of loss, as the old pantomime dispersed, or whenever school broke up and the playing fields stood empty in the evening's afterglow and I thought of all I had known there only a day or two since, and everybody somewhere in a void tonight.

The problem faced by young Cardus was commonplace enough, and so was his reaction to it. Either Bamforth or one of Bamforth's business rivals

The Bijou Magic Lantern and Slides.

If You Were The Only Girl In The World (1).

Sometimes when I feel bad and things look blue,
I wish a girl I had—say one like you;
Someone within my heart to build her throne,
Someone who'd never part, to call my own.
I'll try a love to teach, dear, fond and true,
I sigh a world to reach, dear, just made for me and you.

BAMFORTH COPYRIGHT   WORDS BY PERMISSION OF B. FELDMAN & CO

If You Were The Only Girl In The World (2).

If I were the only girl in the world, and you were the only boy,
Nothing else would matter in the world to-day, we could go on
loving in the same old way;
A Garden of Eden, just made for two, with nothing to mar our joy,
I would say such wonderful things to you, there would be such
wonderful things to do,
If I were the only girl in the world, and you were the only boy.

BAMFORTH COPYRIGHT   WORDS BY PERMISSION OF B. FELDMAN & CO

I'LL TAKE YOU HOME AGAIN, KATHLEEN. No. 2.
(REFRAIN.)

Oh! I will take you back, Kathleen,
To where your heart will feel no pain;
And when the fields are fresh and green,
I'll take you to your home again.

DON'T FORGET MIGNONETTE (1).

In a little garden fair walked a youth so lonely,
Gazing at a floweret there he remarked "I love you only;"
There were blossoms proud and tall, Orchids 'neath a glass shone splendour,
Still he loved her best of all, whispering those words so tender.

WORDS BY PERMISSION OF SHAPIRO VON TILZER MUSIC CO., LTD.
PHOTO ONLY COPYRIGHT 1909.
BY BAMFORTH & CO.

Cards like these provided some solace to star-struck admirers at the turn of the century

offered a palliative to that pain which Cardus could not define:

When at last the pantomime came to an end winter was changing to spring. On the Monday following the last performance on a Saturday night, I was a wandering spirit. The theatre was closed, and I walked about the streets, melancholy in the twilight. The cloud-capped towers and the gorgeous palaces, the great globe itself, had dissolved. The principal girl whose portrait on a post-card I had carried in my pocket since Christmas, until the edges frayed, was far away in London, rehearsing for a George Edwardes' musical comedy. Eugene Stratton was top of the bill at the Hippodrome in Newcastle. The Fairy Queen had returned to her home in Balham, where her invalid mother lived. On the front page of The Era *was a brief statement to the effect that the Demon King was 'resting' in Acacia Road or Maida Vale.*

Throughout the range of post-Victorian reminiscence, there can surely exist few more poignant testimonies to the useful function of the decorative postcard, and it would hardly have occurred to a naïve and satisfied customer like young Cardus that Bamforth and his professional contemporaries might be running into type-casting problems. Certainly there was something risible about, say, Miss Hannah Hinchcliffe, who had 'an innocent, pure look and was often shown clasping a bible, looking demurely to Heaven', also starring in tableaux of a rather more secular nature, in which she was seen kissing young Master Edwin. But it was young Master Edwin who now came up with the great masterstroke. Having realised that with a little judicious marketing the comic postcard might be made an indispensable adjunct of the seaside holiday, he saw that one way of not having to kiss the pietistic Miss Hinchcliffe any more was to dispense with live models altogether and employ cartoon artists instead. The stage was finally set for the apotheosis of the saucy postcard.

The mute inglorious Leonardos of the Bamforth revolution were artists like Douglas Tempest and Arnold Taylor, who between them created the Bamforth comic card ambience. Tempest stayed with Bamforth's from 1911 to 1952, and it is the central period of his career with them which embodies the second, far greater golden age of the British postcard. The statistics really are quite extraordinary. A single card might sell as many as five or six million copies, tickling the fancy in Southport, nudging the funnybone in Yarmouth. If it were a popular item, it might remain in circulation for as long as twenty years, until the young blades who had originally ogled and giggled and smirked at its outrageous presumptions had long since congealed into worried middle-aged men, themselves worried about the lecherous tendencies of their own sons. By the end of the 1930s the idea of an English seaside resort without vulgar postcards was unthinkable. You might as well try to conjure the image of the seaside without ice-cream, or donkeys, or the crunching of brown brogues on pebbles, or eroded sand-castles, or lost buckets and rusting spades, or the fine lace filigree of the pier standing out against scudding spoilsport clouds. The postcards were not to be avoided. You found them in newsagents' shops, hanging among back numbers of *Dalton's Weekly* and *Picture Post*, or wedged between dusty bottles of cough candy and acid drops. You encountered them again at the chemists' shops, mingling incongruously with cheap sunglasses, toothbrushes with transparent handles and podgy tubes of anti-blistering cream. You even found yourself face to face with the cards in the open street, where they stood sentinel in metal racks, so that you could literally not stroll along the pavement without catching their garish chromatic tones, or even, if you reduced your speed, savouring the leering lechery of their boldly printed captions. They constituted a sub-culture so vast and all-pervading that there could have been no member of the great mass of the British working classes who was not intimately familiar with its conventions. This is not to say that everybody approved; there is no puritanism more rampant than the puritanism which stands defiant in a sea of proletarian vulgarity, and I can recall at least two landladies of my experience who disapproved most acidulously. But whether approving or not, everyone was aware of the choice. The vulgar postcards were as vital a piece in the jigsaw of daily life as the pint of beer or the packet of fags, as the racing edition of *The Star* and the placards displaying the coming week's attractions at the local Odeon or Gaumont.

And yet when the vulgar postcard finally received the ultimate intellectual accolade, from George Orwell in 1941, it was with an air of sensational discovery. In discussing the art of Donald McGill, the star artist of Bamforth's rivals the Pictorial Postcard Company, Orwell begins with a rhetorical question: *Who does not know . . . the penny or twopenny coloured post cards with their endless succession of fat women in tight bathing dresses and their crude drawing and unbearable colours?*

But he goes on to say, 'It is a curious fact that many

THIS IS THE PLACE TO TICKLE YOUR FANCY!

Donald McGill's work spanned 40 years of postcards

people seem to be unaware of these things'. Orwell was certainly mistaken; what he must have meant was that the cards had not figured heavily in his own early experience. This is often a difficulty in assessing Orwell's perspicuity in treating cultural themes not previously considered worthy of any kind of analytical treatment. It would be excessively churlish to deny his vital perception that there existed a gulf between what the academics considered to be culture and what the mass of people took for their cultural sustenance. But in his review of the art of Donald McGill, as indeed in his attempt to trace crypto-fascist tendencies in Billy Bunter and Bertie Wooster, there is an unmistakable hint in Orwell's attitude and responses of a man who has come late, on an intellectual ticket, to themes which everyone else has experienced at a much earlier, purely intuitive stage of experience.

Even so, the McGill essay is justly renowned for its symbolic gesture of recognition towards mass culture, and contains several insights into the morality of the vulgar postcard. Characteristically Orwell, with his neat, reasoned paragraphs and his unflappable critical intelligence, finds the one paradoxical truth at the heart of the postcard world, with its pendulous breasts and uplifted skirts, its rampant virgins and slyly self-abusing schoolboys. He is describing one of the stock newly-wed jokes, where the bridegroom gets out of bed after the wedding night, saying to his partner, 'I'll go and get the milk and papers and bring you a cup of tea'; an inset shows the doorstep cluttered with four newspapers and four bottles of milk. Orwell continues:

This is obscene, if you like, but it is not immoral. Its implication – and this is just the implication the Esquire *or* New Yorker *would avoid at all costs – is that marriage is something profoundly exciting and important, the biggest event in the average human being's life.*

In fact the kind of card-situation he is discussing is really implying that it is not marriage itself but the sexual consummation of marriage which is 'profoundly exciting and important'. But Orwell is quite right about the morality, because the vulgar postcard also implies that if the dream of unbridled sex is what secretly preoccupies us all it is a dream not to be fulfilled without the ball-and-chain of the marriage contract.

The truth which emerges from this critical scrutiny is indeed a joke far richer than anything to be found in the cards themselves. For we can now see that the

vulgar postcard depended for its life's blood on the survival of that mealy-mouthed puritanism which it derided. Like the salacious pietism of those Sunday newspapers which purse their lips in bogus disapproval even as they boost circulation, the randiness of the vulgar postcard was an adjunct of respectability, of self-denial, of decorum, and we wonder what place there would be for it in a world completely won over by the clinical self-indulgences of the Permissive Age. The work of men like McGill and Tempest and Taylor was a response to the yearnings of a ludicrously buttoned-up society, a mass of people baffled and angered by the alarming hypocritical discrepancies between society's rules and their own appetites. Only a crackpot would deny that the British working classes enjoy making jokes about sex and are inclined, to borrow Orwell's phrase, to blow a raspberry at those moralists who try to forbid them to do so. Until the 1960s, little of this ribald sexual humour ever found its way into print, which is why the social historian of the future, ferreting around in the files to discover the pivot of working-class smalltalk, will ferret in vain. Only in the world of the vulgar postcard will he catch a glimpse of the innuendo which continues to hang like a drunken halo over the heads of the proletariat.

Enemies of the vulgar postcard have said that the whole business is crude and obscene, and that its *dramatis personae* are brutalised to the brink of imbecility. I will not make the same tactical mistake as some defendants of Marie Lloyd used to make back in the Edwardian period. To have denied Marie's vulgarity would have been to question her efficacy as an artist. Marie was vulgar because she was a genius who worked hard all her life to master the art of vulgarity. For the same reason the vulgar postcard is

Max Miller, the music hall's answer to saucy postcard humour

BEHAVE YOURSELF, SANDY!

"I COULD ENJOY MYSELF HERE - BUT........"

"I COULD HAVE HAD A PLEASANT TIME BUT"

"I'VE GOT A B(U)OY AT LAST - BUT........"

"THE VOYAGE WAS GLORIOUS - BUT......."

"Things Went Down Alright-
BUT_____"

"They Would Have Been Nibbling-
BUT_____"

"I Was Beginning to Enjoy Myself Here
BUT_____"

"I Should Have Been Gloomy Here
BUT_____"

crude and brutalised, because that is its intention. What is more to the point is that the vulgar postcard is not pornographic. The human being does not exist who could ever be sexually excited by the art of McGill and company. Orwell felt that the postcards represented a skit on pornography, but the evidence suggests that they are something quite different, a skit on eroticism. They are a lampoon of conventional appetites, a reduction to absurdity of those submerged desires of the male for self-supporting breasts and the kind of protruding bottoms which leave a room several seconds after their owners, a caricature of what the young man's fancy turns to at every available opportunity. What we find in these drawings is not reality but a derisive projection of reality. The distinction is a vital one, because it makes clear the presence in the captions of a certain element of wit. It may be a low wit, a crude wit, a regrettable wit, a wit to be spurned by the Podsnaps of this world, but it is a wit for all that, just as Mae West's pelvic dialogue is wit and Max Miller's gutter facetiousness is wit. Both West and Miller are relevant to the argument, for the hips of one and the quips of the other transmuted into real life what the postcards depicted in art. Miller in particular was a three-dimensional, walking, talking vulgar postcard, an artist whose material often coincides to a striking degree with the captions in this anthology. There is an early Bamforth card showing a courting couple at the Zoo; an elephant has thrust its trunk through the bars of its cage and touched the young lady on the shoulder, an endearment to which she responds with 'Oh Horace, you are a dear'. In Miller's version, flung defiantly from the stage of the old Metropolitan Music Hall in the Edgware Road, a young lady washing clothes at the riverside is tapped on the behind by that same elephant and without looking round she remarks, with the perspicacity of the born hedonist, 'Mister, I don't know who you are, but I'm here every Tuesday and Thursday morning.'

In spite of the twentieth century's violent reaction to the old discredited Victorian prudery, the vulgar postcard retains its hold on the sensibilities of the general public to a surprising degree, adding to its stock of *double entendre* any new clichés which happen to come along – so that the lusty young lady, asked what she thinks of UNO, takes the opportunity to reply, 'I never think of anything else'. Such candours no longer seem as scandalous as they once did, but so disastrous and far-reaching were the effects of the old evasions and hypocrisies that it will be some time yet before the British feel liberated enough to require no longer the retaliatory weapon of the bawdy postcard. And in any case, a few pockets of resistance are bound to survive; one of the more contemporary Bamforth cards shows some aldermanic Mrs Grundy opening a youth club with the words, 'We want this place to be run by a person who knows what the teenagers want to do – but old enough to see they don't do it'. In a famous declaration of discontent, Thackeray once grumbled that *Since the author of* Tom Jones *was buried, no writer of fiction among us has been permitted to depict to his utmost powers a man . . . You will not hear what moves in the real world, what passes in society, in the clubs, colleges, mess-rooms, what is the life and talk of your sons.* Substitute for the clubs, colleges and mess-rooms of Thackeray's world the pubs, factories and men's rooms of our own, and the vulgar postcard goes a considerable way towards supplying the deficiency which so troubled the author of *Vanity Fair* (although not so strongly that he ever felt inclined to do anything about it).

In the years since Thackeray died, the average young British male has continued to discuss with the informed preoccupation of the connoisseur the curve of a breast and the line of a buttock, the odds against conception and the relationship, if any, between the dimensions of the pudenda and the prowess of its owner. Censorship has been against it, although the curious truth remains that even the most repressive Lord Chamberlain began life as the outcome of one of those sexual acts whose existence he has pretended not to notice. Our Betters have been against it, although the even more curious fact remains that they were against it in others rather than in themselves. School-teachers and academics have been against it, even though their moral leader Dr Bowdler was perhaps after all not the most trustworthy guide in such matters. Forgetting for the moment our Censors and our Betters and our Improvers, and concentrating instead on the spectacle of the British pursuing their own ends and each other's, let us see what passed through the mails.

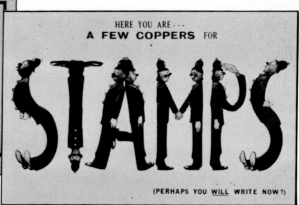

2
BESIDE THE SEASIDE

When the steel web of the railway began to spread across the face of newly industrialised England, and the fashion for the old Georgian spa was eclipsed by that magnificent high Victorian institution, the Seaside, the English entered into one of their great Rabelaisian interludes. The coming of cheap travel was a mixed blessing, dealing a death-blow to the traditions of old rural England. Previously a rustic from the Wiltshire hills might have talked of 'going up to town' and meant Salisbury, and the authentic Cornish Pasty never crossed the path of the Yarmouth Bloater or the Arbroath Smokie. Before the coming of the cheap day-excursion and the annihilation of distance, England was, socially speaking, a loose-knit confederacy of counties and customs, a land where everything from language to the militia was set in a regional mould. The novels of Thomas Hardy and Eden Phillpots are thronged with characters who live out their lives without ever seeing the sea.

Indeed, the very tensions of the Victorian plot were often created by the valiant attempts of the embattled hero to reach the sea, where, some instinct told him, his salvation surely lay. When young Copperfield trudges from Blackfriars to Dover, subsidising his forlorn expedition by selling his clothing as he goes, the reader breathes a sigh of compassionate relief when Dickens's favourite child at last finds his nostrils tickled by the brine of the English Channel. By then Davey was already on nodding terms with the idea that the seashore was commensurate with liberation, having spent an idyllic interlude at Yarmouth, where the town and the tide were 'mixed up like toast and water'. But Dickens knew also the less melodramatic, more uproarious and purely hedonistic aspect of the matter. The first thing his Mr Tuggs does on coming into £20,000 is to invade Ramsgate, where, on arriving

HAVING A CHEAP HOLIDAY HERE, BUT MAKING THE MOST OF IT

CHAIR 1ᵈ

Lowestoft, 1900

at the pier, he surveys the glorious recreational scene before him:

The sun was shining brightly; the sea, dancing to its own music, rolled merrily in; crowds of people promenaded to and fro; young ladies tittered; old ladies talked; nursemaids displayed their charms to the greatest possible advantage; and their little charges ran up and down, and to and fro, and in and out, under the feet, and between the legs, of the assembled concourse, in the most playful and exhilarating manner. There were old gentlemen, trying to make out objects through long telescopes; and young ones, making objects of themselves in open shirt-collars; ladies carrying about portable chairs, and portable chairs carrying about invalids; parties, waiting on the pier for parties who had come by the steamboat, and nothing was to be head but talking, laughing, welcoming, and merriment.

The Tuggses are suitably encouraged, but next morning, when they review the situation down on the sands, it is to discover that they have as yet hardly

glimpsed the true extent of the pleasures of the littoral life:

There were the same ladies and gentlemen, the same children, the same nursemaids, the same telescopes, the same portable chairs. The ladies were employed in needlework, or watch-guard making, or knitting, or reading novels; the gentlemen were reading newspapers and magazines; the children were digging holes in the sand with wooden spades, and collecting water therein; the nursemaids, with their youngest charges in their arms, were running in after the waves, and then running back with the waves after them; and, now and then, a little sailing-boat either departed with a gay and talkative cargo of passengers, or returned with a very silent and particularly uncomfortable looking one.

The hypnotic attraction, not of the land or the sea, but of that siren compromise between the two, the beach, continued to hold most Victorian writers after Dickens. Down the perspective of the years we glimpse the Walrus and the Carpenter, who

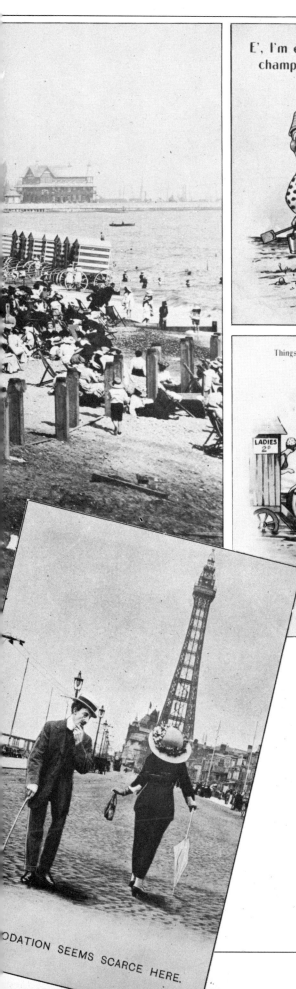

ODATION SEEMS SCARCE HERE.

E', I'm enjoying myself champion

And you wont cop me coming home in a hurry either.

Things are a lot cheaper here, let me tell you!

LADIES 2ᴰ

By gum! I'm enjoying myself, and not 'arf

I dont want to come home. I know that.

By gum, lass, we shan't come here another year—the air's too strong for me!

Wept like anything to see
Such quantities of sand

and the insomniac Lord Chancellor who, when at last he does fall asleep, prefers insomnia after all, for

You dream you are crossing the Channel, and tossing about in a steamer from Harwich,
Which is something between a large bathing-machine and a very small second-class carriage.

W. S. Gilbert's reference to that archetypal Victorian symbol, the bathing-machine, is a reminder that there was something else about the discovery of the seaside which in a sense was the most vital aspect of all, an aspect utterly remote from the conventional considerations, from the ozone and the white horses of the surf, from rampant landladies and the egg-timer's damp sand on the parlour mantelpiece. This most significant factor was one of the great revelations of the Industrial Age, a mighty upheaval in social history, a great tribal surge along the road to liberation. For the Victorian working classes, having arrived at the ragged fringes of the surf, were delighted to discover that there was something about going in the water which was not covered by biblical edicts and municipal constrictions, something whose full implications had never been considered at all. You had to take all your clothes off.

It is perfectly true that a great many of the Victorians, having taken all their clothes off, immediately put on a fresh set just as impenetrable. This lunatic exchange was performed behind the ramparts of a waterlogged box called a bathing-machine, into which

landlocked crinoline and starch disappeared through one door and emerged five minutes later from another, transformed into what looks, to contemporary eyes, like the residue of a carpet sale. But as the years went by and the scandalously prurient modesty of our great-grandfathers became eroded by advancing tides of sanity, so the safety-line retreated. After Mr Tuggs, the Plimsoll Line of respectability inexorably rose above the ankle, above the calf, above the knee, above the thigh, ever onward and upward towards the Rabelaisian ideal of the Birthday Suit.

Now the great thing about relaxing the rules is to let others, less fortunate, know what they are missing. So once you arrived at the seaside, once you had flung your woollen socks and your flannel shirt to the winds and bared your milk-white body to the breeze, your first act was to write home and imply that the

ARE YOU READY?
I WISH YOU WERE GOING IN WITH ME

moment you stepped off that excursion train all sorts of not quite respectable things had happened, or were happening, or were surely about to happen at any moment. The transmission of this message was more than a pleasure; it was a positive duty. Almost before you had unpacked and crossed swords for the first time with your landlady, out you went to the nearest newsagent's, clambered over the buckets and spades and the bottled sweets, snatched up a handful of the most vulgar and disgustingly coarse postcards you could find, scribbled something suitably coy on the back, and posted them off to suburbia, where the early-morning postman, armoured against shock by the length of his own experience, calmly dropped the epistolary bombshells on to the doormats of respectability and went on his way. 'Having a wonderful time,' said the message, 'wish you were here.'

Wish you were where? What kind of world was to be discovered in those postcards? The first thing you noticed was that within its boundaries certain alarm-

ing amendments had been made to the human anatomy. Female breasts, for instance, became less like breasts than the twin ramparts of a well-endowed battleship. Moreover, they were ramparts which never ever wilted, breasts which defied the laws of Newtonian physics with splendid consistency and proved once and for all that Einstein was right when he said that the shortest distance between two points is very often curved. There was something else rather curious about these breasts. It was clear that in the wake of matrimony and the formalising of sin into marital duty, these breasts, in the fullness of time and the Saloon Bar, congealed into a vast pampas of bosom. In the world of the comic postcard there is no intermediary stage between saucy girl-friend and irascible wife. Even more alarming, the young blade of courting days shrinks into the browbeaten dishwasher of middle age. The male grows steadily smaller, as the wife grows steadily larger, almost as though there were some kind of law of inverse proportion in operation which science knows nothing about. The parity of the sexual hunt ends as an extraordinary and totally unfair guerrilla war between a male Lilliput and an indomitable female Brobdingnag.

It is understood that inside the world of comic postcards everybody, whether male or female, goes to the seaside either to participate in, or to think about, or to watch out for, one thing. And as that one thing remained throughout the nineteenth century unmentionable in polite society, certainly in anything as

open as the public postal service, and was hardly to be thought about until even the dissolute twentieth century was more than half over, it followed that a certain code was required for the successful smuggling across the frontiers of respectability of those disgraceful and disturbing messages to suburbia. The code was based on the deliberate confusion of semantics, a confusion which reached its crowning glory with the one-line *double entendre* of the filthy-clean postcard. The caption-writers, having been handed a batch of portraits featuring dream-breasts and nightmare-bosoms, marshalled their arsenal of ambiguity and euphemism and began matching the lasciviousness of the eye with the lewdness of the word.

They soon discovered that the location of a submarine's periscope is roughly analogous to the location on a man's body of a different kind of protuberance. They also remembered from their childhood that the word 'wind' may or may not refer to climatic conditions. Once the human mind, being the regrettably coarse device it undoubtedly is, starts to think along these lines, the possibilities are very nearly endless. A girl who finds herself in deep water, for example, may never have strayed from the esplanade. The chap who approaches a young lady who happens to be eating candyfloss and asks her if she has any objection to his 'having a bit' may often end up enjoying something rather more substantial than a mouthful of sticky gauze.

But the hint of sexual liberation which the seaside

THERE'S NO HOLDING ME DOWN HERE!
THIS IS ME GOING HOME FOR MY
DINNER

SPENT UP! IF THE DONKEY CAN MANAGE
IT I'M COMING HOME LIKE THIS

HAVING MY ANNUAL

ENJOY YOURSELF LIKE
HELEN B. MERRY!
THAT'S OUR MOTTO HERE

postcards contain was after all only part of the truth. The sea represented for the English masses a more profound liberation; it was something commensurate with their sense of wonder, and it represented an expansiveness whose very existence might easily be forgotten in the labyrinth of back streets in which the urban poor lived out their lives. Somehow anything seemed possible in sight of the sea, and sexual dalliance was only one of several departures which struck the mind at the moment when ozone hit the nostrils. The greatest creative artist that the late Victorian working classes ever produced has recorded his sentiments at the moment when he gazed for the first time on the ocean, at a watering place called Southend-on-Sea:

My first sight of the sea was hypnotic. As I approached it in bright sunlight from a hilly street, it looked suspended, a live quivering monster about to fall on me. The three of us took off our shoes and paddled. The tepid sea

THIS IS ME AN' OUR EMMANUEL GOING FOR OUR ANNUAL

Mind you don't bump into a submarine, Auntie.

unfurling over my insteps and around my ankles and the soft yielding sand under my feet were a revelation of delight. What a day that was – the saffron beach, with its pink and blue pails and wooden spades, its coloured tents and umbrellas, and sailing boats hurtling gaily over laughing little waves, and up on the beach other boats resting idly on their sides, smelling of seaweed and tar – the memory of it still lingers with enchantment.

There are two points worth observing in that tiny tone-poem from the autobiography of Charlie Chaplin. First, the sense of exhilaration which we have already noted in the impact of Ramsgate upon the sensibilities of Dickens, and second, the ruthless way in which the chromatic prettifications which Chaplin remembers, the pails and spades, the sea and the sand,

JUST A LINE! I'M NOT MARKED WITH A CROSS...
YOU'LL HAVE TO GUESS WHICH IS ME

HERE WE ARE AGAIN. BOW-LEGS, KNOCK-KNEES AND
HAIRY-LEGS - - - WHICH IS ME?

are ruthlessly over-simplified by the postcard artists to serve their purpose of broad innuendo. In the cards we may spot the occasional smiling donkey, the occasional smirking starfish, the occasional saucy crab. But any trace of the sentiment which so affected Chaplin is absent from the seaside of the postcards. What does remain in common between the two is this sense of expansiveness which the sea-shore apparently lends to the English; for Chaplin the expansiveness of a life of vague promise, for the postcard artists the expansiveness of an endless permissiveness.

The seaside postcard is different from all the others for two very important reasons; first, because it necessarily features people in various stages of undress, and second, because it catches people in a situation where the despatching of a postcard home is one of the imperatives of existence. After the railways made it possible to contemplate the possibility of a dirty weekend at Margate or Brighton or Morecambe or Felixstowe or even, dare one suspect, Eastbourne, there was further encouragement to follow the road to enjoyable ruin – the Bank Holiday Act of 1871, the arrival of the motor-car, and above all the devastation of distance which made the furtive art of the chaperon *passé*. The realist may point out, and he is probably right, that your dedicated seaboard sinner is so busy sea-board-sinning that he has no time to browse through the randy pastures of the comic postcards,

and that the ones who do are the true innocents. It is the merely vicarious lustpots who have the leisure to make a fetish of the fat lady up to her bosom in crabs or the small boy in the shallows holding one hand aloft waving the Union Jack and the other hand submerged, holding something we dare not think about and saying, with smug joy, 'What we have, we hold'. If disbarred by their own temperaments from playing a leading role in the sexual comedy, they can at least sit back and get a laugh out of those who do. Perhaps years later our eternal spectator comes across one of his own cards, lying forgotten among the dry grains of yesterday's sand at the bottom of an ancient suitcase. He picks it up and dusts it off, reads his own jocose message, contemplates the remarkable outlines of the young lady on the other side, and replaces the card with a smile, hearing in his imagination the brassy voice of recollection:

Oh, I do like to be beside the seaside,
Oh, I do like to be beside the sea

and smirking at the recollection of *why* he liked to be beside it. The reality never quite lived up to the promise of the postcards, but no matter. And at least he did manage, once upon a time, to get to the sea while still unspoken for. He cannot quite remember now how he got there, whether by train, or car, or tandem bicycle, or even on foot, but then, one of the advantages of having been a child of the twentieth century is that there are so many different ways of getting from A to B, each of them more convenient than the others.

MOSTLY MOTOR BOATS THESE DAYS
BUT IT'S NICE TO SEE
RED SAILS IN THE SUNSET
FOR A CHANGE !

"YOU FATHEAD — **YOU DON'T NEED
TO ADVERTISE IT—WE'RE
NOT BLIND !"**

"I KNOW IT'S THE BREAST STROKE, BUT I WANT YOU
TO HOLD ME **UNDER THE CHIN !"**

3
TRANSPORTS OF DELIGHT

With regard to the comic postcard treatment of modes of transport, the one vital fact which needs to be kept firmly in the forefront of the mind is that it is very nearly impossible to copulate on a horse. In a horse, yes, as the Greeks of Odysseus may well have discovered before the walls of Troy, but not on one. It is very doubtful if anyone has managed this feat since the days of Attila the Hun, but then Attila the Hun actually lived on his horse, and as the American humorist Will Cuppy has observed, look what happened there. The modern world, preoccupied with its gaskets and its oil strikes, tends to take the internal combustion engine for granted. We forget that up until the other day, in terms of sidereal time, it was impossible to travel at a speed greater than our feet would take us without the willing co-operation of a horse. Now the interesting thing about a horse is that it is virtually impossible to

conceal one about your person, so that a chaperon wouldn't notice. Therefore, in the days before the internal combustion engine, it was doubly difficult for the sly seducer and the furtive fornicator to practise their arts undetected.

Throughout the nineteenth century various inventions appeared on the market whose concerted effect was to render the function of the chaperon obsolete, and to make it progressively easier for young males and females to absent themselves from the prying eyes of their elders, in order to perform certain acts which they could never have dreamed of achieving while galloping along on a horse. This new development began with the railway, intensified with the motor-car, became uncontrollable with the bicycle, and finally assumed the proportions of a universal orgy with the aeroplane. Indeed, it is a simple task, even for a professional sociologist, to trace the interrelationship of cheap travel and free love through the landmarks of the last 150 years.

The professional chaperon, realising that the more mobile people became the more impractical it would be to police them, must have experienced the first faint twinges of apprehension in September 1830, when a politician called William Huskisson attended the official opening of the Liverpool and Manchester Railway only to find himself inadvertently attending his own official closing, his spectacular role in the proceedings being reported in all the newspapers the next day – in the obituary columns. The incident no doubt furnished Charles Dickens eighteen years later with a suitably melodramatic way of getting rid of Carker in *Dombey and Son*. To James Carker belongs the dubious honour of being the first major character in English fiction to arrive in Heaven by railway, for, stumbling off the platform, he was:

beaten down, caught up, and whirled away upon a jagged mill, that spun him round and round, and struck him limb from limb, and licked his stream of life up with its fiery heat, and cast his mutilated fragments in the air.

By 1875 Tolstoy was arranging for Anna Karenina to end her life by flinging herself under a passing train, by 1890 Zola was devoting an entire novel, *La Bête Humaine*, to the innovation of the railway, and before the end of the century the Iron Horse had finally been apotheosized by Oscar Wilde, who built an immortal tissue of moonshine round the premise that a man might start out in life as an item in a railway Left Luggage office and still prove to be a gentleman. Most important of all, the development of the railway added a new dimension to the art of lovemaking, for while a pair of unmarried lovers, if they stayed at a hotel, had to go through the Mr and Mrs Smith rigmarole, they could book a sleeper to Edinburgh and nobody would dream of asking to see their marriage lines. It is surprising that the following exchange has never taken place in an English Divorce Court:

Judge : How many times did you spend the night with the defendant?

Woman : Only once.

Judge : Where did adultery take place?

Woman : If it please your Lordship, it was in Herts, Beds, Northants, Lincs, Yorkshire, Durham and Northumberland.

Not only overnight trains to Scotland, but on a more modest level the gradual introduction of cheap fares, Day Excursions and Seaside Specials, meant that more and more young people were finding it less and less difficult to escape the attentions of those watchdogs which society provided for the express

Seaside Specials meant cheap travel – for an annual outing or a week or two away

purpose of keeping the incidence of virginity as high as was humanly possible, and perhaps even higher. But of equal significance was the Bank Holiday legislation which provided the proletariat with something of which it had been vouchsafed precious little – spare time. Somerset Maugham was careful in his first novel, *Liza of Lambeth* (1897), to ascribe his heroine's loss of honour to a Bank Holiday outing to Chingford, and to tell us later that when Liza is living with her Jim she notices on his mantelpiece those symbols of past escapades, cups and saucers advertising the legend 'A Present from Clacton-on-Sea' or 'A Memento from Margate'. One reads those phrases and catches a faint echo of an old music hall song which harped on the same theme:

It wasn't the girl I saw you with at Brighton,
Who were you with last night?

However, there are more ways than one of getting to Brighton, and if the railway gave the would-be lecher a heaven-sent mobility, and also to some extent the anonymity of being a visitor to a strange town, it was the motor-car which gave him something even more precious – privacy. At first the little tin gods who manufactured the little Tin Lizzies quite mistook the nature of the revolution they had engendered, believing in their innocence that a motor-car was purely a means of transport, and not the transport of delight it subsequently proved to be. In 1919 the penny had not yet dropped; only one American automobile in ten had a roof. Five years later the figure had risen to 43 per cent, and by 1927 to 82 per cent. One social historian has noted the dawning realisation in the ranks of the amorous that:

the closed car was in effect a room protected from the weather which could be moved at will into a darkened byway or a country lane.

In the same study, *Middletown*, is also recorded the fact that, when one small-town judge examined the cases of thirty young ladies brought before him on charges of indecency, he discovered that nineteen of them had been doing whatever it was they had been doing in the *sanctum sanctorum* of a closed motor-car. The trend was most perfectly expressed in a cartoon which Peter Arno drew for *The New Yorker*, and which the editor, Harold Ross, published only because he possessed too much horse-and-buggy innocence to understand it. In Arno's cartoon a courting couple walk up to a speed cop and say, 'We want to report a stolen car'. Under his arm the young man is carrying the detachable back seat, which illustrates how conveniently a motor-car could be not only a weather-

Driving to the Derby, 1922

"NOW THEN YOU TWO—WHICH OF YOU IS THE LEARNER?"
L
A BAMFORTH COMIC
IS IT NEARLY TIME FOR THE CAR TO BREAK DOWN, GEORGE?
"I'LL JUS'H SEE IF WAGON TRAIN IS ON THE OTHER CHANNEL, BERT —I'M FED UP WITH THESE SLOPPY LOVE STORIES!"
CU 2
A 'BAMFORTH' COMIC
THE DOUBLE CLUTCH!
"I WANT TO REPORT A STOLEN CAR, CONSTABLE!"
TO THE WOODS
A 'BAMFORTH' COMIC

CHEERIO, OLD BEAN, I'VE **CLICKED**!
AND NOT WITH A HIKER, OH, NO!

"YOU WON'T LET US GO TOO FAR, WILL
  YOU, CONDUCTOR?"
"NOT LIKELY! —IV'E BEEN WATCHING
  YOU FOR A BIT!"

IF YOU LIKE SWEETS, ONE TART'S NOTHING—FIT THE
EXTENSION PILLION AND HAVE A TRAY FULL!

THE LATEST MODEL, AND ITS ADVANTAGES:—
COMFORT WHILE WAITING FOR ROBOTS TO CHANGE TO GREEN.
THIRD PARTY INSURANCE UNDER THE PILLOW, ETC., ETC.

IT'LL COME TO IT SOONER OR LATER,
MOTORISTS HAVE TO DO IT - - - WHY NOT PEDESTRIANS?

SHE IS AN' ALL!

ETHYL IS HERE

I MUST HAVE GOT A COUPLE OF THEM BLESSED AUSTIN SEVENS ON ME!

AGENT FOR AUSTIN SEVENS

SHELL

OK 9365

MISSUS! YER BABY'S LEAKING!

GOSH. 'ERB! ME LUMBAGO'S GIVING ME H—!!

proof room, but also, on balmy nights, a removal van for a makeshift bed of roses.

But the young lovers in Arno's cartoon have that well-scrubbed look about them which implies a tolerable income. The underlings of this world could hardly aspire either to the income or to the four wheels which it could purchase, and so they snatched at the compensation of two wheels. Between the years 1890 and 1910 the safety bicycle, buoyant on its cushion of a perfected inner tube, must have inspired more romances, encouraged more stolen kisses, driven more chaperons to distraction and led to more epistolary indiscretions than there were spokes in the Rudge workshops. In March 1896 we find Bernard Shaw writing a letter of precise bicycling advice to the critic William Archer, explaining that prices for new machines are high 'in consequence of the prodigious boom'. Six months later, Shaw, who had been conducting from the vantage point of his saddle a lightning courtship of the lady soon to be his wife, wrote to his love one of the most passionate letters of the epoch and one which indicates the extent to which the young romancers of the period depended on the mobility afforded to them by their machines:

Dear Charlotte,
The enclosed belongs to your bicycle pump. I forgot to

give it to you. What a lonely evening, and cold going to bed.

GBS.

In that same year, while Shaw was philandering among the Fabians in the hedgerows of southern England, his world-bettering friend H. G. Wells was preparing for publication a novel pointedly called *The Wheels of Chance*, whose hero, even more pointedly called Hoopdriver, is the archetype of the blotchy, unfulfilled lower middle-class menial who sets out on his annual fortnight's holiday from the drapery emporium and stumbles on the promise of true love thanks only to his possession of a bicycle. But neither Shaw nor Wells was as quick to record the implications for morality of the bicycling explosion as the actor-writer George Grossmith, who, four years before, had published *The Diary of a Nobody*. In that accidental masterpiece Mr Pooter, most memorable of suburban husbands, confides to his diary the friendly gesture of Cummings, most memorable of suburban bachelors:

April 27 : Cummings said he couldn't stop, he only called to leave me the Bicycle News, *as he had done with it.*

A few days later Pooter, Cummings and their friend Gowings decide to take a Sunday morning walk, which brings us to the one form of propulsion requir-

SOMETHING TELLS ME IT'S HER BIG END, LAD!

GOSH BILL! IF THE BLINKING OLD LORRY HASN'T STARTED TO LAY!

"DO YE KNOW THE DIFFERENCE BETWEEN A TRAM AND A TAXI, MAGGIE?"
"NO, SANDY!"
"RIGHT, WE'LL GO BY TRAM, THEN!"

YOUR NAME'S ROBERT, ISN'T IT, DADDY? WERE THE **ROBOTS** NAMED AFTER **YOU**?

"DO YOU REALLY WANT TO SEE MY LICENSE, CONSTABLE?"
"NO! I'VE SEEN ENOUGH!"

"I'VE JUST PICKED HER UP—ALL SHE NEEDS IS HER **BOTTOM RUBBERISING**!"

"I'LL GIVE 'EM A TRIAL GERTIE— CASCARA DOESN'T DO ME ANY GOOD!"

"QUICK, DOCTOR, HIS EYES ARE POPPING OUT AND HE'S CHOKING—SHALL I LOOSEN HIS COLLAR?"
"NO, MISS—**JUST FASTEN YOURS UP**!"

"YOU WALKED ACROSS AS THOUGH YOU WERE BLIND!"
"MAY BE, MAY BE—BUT I'M NOT BLIND NOW, MISS!"

ENJOYING OURSELVES TO SOME TUNE HERE

Unbridled jollity on a char-a-banc outing in 1925

ELLIMAN'S REMOVES STIFFNESS

NO STIFFNESS HERE THANKS TO ELLIMAN

wise debarred by the proprieties from flashing their thighs in public strode about the countryside in the shortest of shorts, confident in the knowledge that before long there would be something a bit more useful than a porpoise close behind them.

Here lies the essence of the postcard artist's reaction to the boom in mass mobility which marks the social history of the last hundred years. All the new modes of transport seemed to demand in the most delightful way the protuberance of those parts of the anatomy most conducive to a bit of slap-and-tickle. The man who follows a young lady up the stairs to the top deck of a bus very quickly learns to appreciate the wisdom of Robert Louis Stevenson's remark about it being better to travel than to arrive. Young ladies who balance themselves with feline precision on bicycle saddles, or who ride pillion on motor-bikes, must learn not to be put out when the male bystander flings shafts of wit concerning gearsticks and starting handles. For the truth is that underlying the moving of the human being from A to B is a vague conviction in his breast that somehow to be a moving target removes all the usual sanctions. There are no action replays in real life and, provided the actors move fast enough, nobody can ever be quite sure he saw them do what he thought he saw them do. The rule applies even at the most mundane of levels, as Max Miller proved when he mounted a London omnibus and pleaded with the conductress to be allowed to ride even though he had no money. She, foolish virgin, replied, 'Do you want to get me into trouble?' 'Right,' says Max, 'what time do you finish?' It was a conversational exchange which could never have happened had it not been for a cataclysmic event which obliged the British to grapple with the idea of lady bus-conductors.

ing no co-operation from anything or anybody. If the ever-resourceful working classes found that they could not operate effectively in a train, or in a car, or on a bicycle, there was always Shanks's pony. Between the two world wars young people developed the habit of hoisting a rucksack on to their backs and pointing knobbly knees at the nearest range of hills. It was a healthy pastime, to be sure, but the forgotten poet who contributed to the movement the line 'I'm happy when I'm hiking' must have known that a great many of the hikers were also very happy when they stopped hiking and flopped into the bountiful arms of a lush hedge. The great thing was that in dressing for a good walk you were already halfway to being un-dressed for an even better rest. Young ladies other-

BY 'EVE THERE WILL BE ANOTHER FALL

A FLY IN THE SKY
IS WORTH TWO IN THE EYE

Well, if this happens when crows fly,
I don't know what I'll do when
everybody's flying!

Na look at that!—and John's in
it, the silly ass, wi' all our 'oliday
money in 'is pocket!

In the days of its innocence, the aeroplane was seen less as a threat to the splendid isolation of our island fortress, than as a kind of mechanical aid to loving, and an invention which, in its take-offs and landings, evoked comparison with certain items of underwear

"IS THAT YOUR HUSBAND, MADAM?"
"DUNNO, - - - THAT DOESN'T LOOK LIKE HIS FACE!"

TWO SMALL PORTS AND I FEEL QUITE SAUCY

"HAS THE MOON COME UP YET, HERBERT?"
"NAY, NAY, MARY; SURELY I DIDN'T SWALLOW THAT!"

Observing the rule that any human discomfiture involving the evacuation of either the bowels, the nostrils or the stomach is fundamentally comic, the postcard artists often fell back on the device of a long and bumpy sea voyage

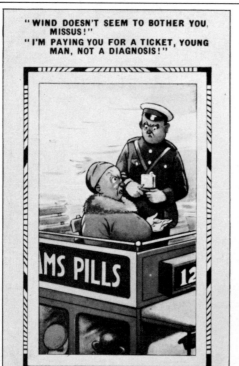

"WIND DOESN'T SEEM TO BOTHER YOU, MISSUS!"
"I'M PAYING YOU FOR A TICKET, YOUNG MAN, NOT A DIAGNOSIS!"

THERE'S SOMETHING ABOUT A SOLDIER!

"GOOD NIGHT, DUCKS! PUT THE CAT OUT AND DON'T BE LATE COMING TO BED!"

4 PRIVATES AT THE FRONT

When the Great War to End Civilisation began on 4 August 1914, the British plunged into it almost as though the fighting was to be an extension of the Bank Holiday they had been celebrating a few hours earlier. A great many innocent fools were overjoyed when the news was announced that the war had begun; at last they would have the opportunity to prove those qualities of manliness in themselves which they appear to have doubted. Rupert Brooke was actually polite enough to say thank you to the Deity for having presented the young men of England with a chance of death, writing, 'Now God be thanked, who has matched us with His Hour', a fragment of surpassing twaddle which conceives the war as a kind of ethical bon-bon, rather like First Fifteen colours only more so. Nor is the analogy too far-fetched, for officers went to France with sporting equipment in their luggage. At Loos in 1915, the

1st Battalion, 18th London Regiment kicked a football at the enemy lines to signal the start of its attack; in an assault on the Turkish lines at Beersheba two years later

One of the men had a football. How it came there goodness knows. Anyway, we kicked off and rushed the first Turkish guns, dribbling the ball with us.

Most extraordinary of all is the behaviour of the officers of the 8th East Surreys at the Battle of the Somme. The American historian Paul Fussell writes: *Captain Nevill, a company commander, bought four footballs, one for each platoon, during his last London leave before the attack. He offered a prize to the platoon which, at the jump-off, first kicked its football up to the German front line. Although J. R. Ackerley remembered Nevill as 'the battalion buffoon', he may have been shrewder than he looked: his little sporting contest did have the effect of persuading his men that that attack*

TO MY PAL

DON'T YOU JUST WISH YOU WERE
HERE 'LONG WITH ME!
THE DRILLING IS FINE, AND THE LIFE
IS FREE,
THE BOYS ARE ALL RIGHT, AND THE
FARE'S NOT BAD,
IT'S REALLY A.1. TO BE TRAINING,
LAD.—*Madeleine St. Clair.*

TO ONE OF
THE BOYS

JUST A WORD, OLD SPORT,
TO SAY I'M A.1.,
AND THE LIFE SEEMS TO SUIT
TO A T.
I'VE GOT MUSCLES GALORE
I NE'ER DREAMED OF BEFORE,
AND MY CHEST HAS INCREASED
INCHES THREE.
I GET 'FITTER' EACH DAY—
FACT I'M REALLY O.K.—
BUT YOU WAIT TILL I GET
THE V.C
Madeleine St. Clair.

was going to be, as the staff had been insisting, a walkover. A survivor observing from a short distance away recalls zero hour : 'As the gunfire died away I saw an infantryman climb onto the parapet of No-Man's-Land, beckoning to others to follow. As he did so he kicked off a football. A good kick. The ball rose and travelled well towards the German line. That seemed to

be the signal to advance.' Captain Nevill was killed instantly. Two of the footballs are preserved today in English museums.

Nearly everyone agreed that the soldiers would be home by Christmas, so you had to be quick if you wanted to get in on the act. Ageing patriots like C. E. Montague of the *Manchester Guardian* were so keen not to miss the fun that they resorted to hair-dye to camouflage the telltale grey streaks, thereby becoming the first heroes in recorded history whose hair turned black overnight from the terror of missing the battle. Readers of *The Times* for 9 August 1914 saw this uplifting item:

At an inquest on the body of Arthur Sydney Evelyn

Annesley, aged 49, formerly a captain in the Rifle Brigade, who committed suicide by flinging himself under a heavy van at Pimlico, the Coroner stated that worry caused by the feeling that he was not going to be accepted for service led him to take his life.

Before we laugh at such innocence, we should perhaps mourn its disappearance from the world we now live in, and marvel at the eagerness of millions to immolate themselves on the pyre of the Imperial ideal. The British were the Games Masters of the world and war, after all, was the greatest game of all. In late August 1914 W. G. Grace published his famous open letter to the cricketers of England:

It is not fitting at a time like the present that able-bodied men should play day after day and pleasure-seekers look on. There are many who are young and able and yet are hanging back. I should like to see all first-class cricketers of suitable age set a good example and come to the help of their country without delay in its hour of need.

The crassness of that letter is a terrifying example of what you get for meddling in affairs which are none of your business, but we should be very careful not to dismiss Dr Grace's appeal as a mere clumsy attempt to help his country, a well-intentioned but perhaps misguided gesture which did at least have some effect on recruiting figures. It did, indeed, and that was what was wrong with it. Far from aiding the war effort, announcements like the good Doctor's had so

ONE HEART, ONE MIND, ONE AIM

Vengeance! Victory! Untarnished Fame!

disastrous an effect on the war machine that they could hardly have been more ingeniously worded had they been written by the Kaiser. What escaped the notice of all the patriots was that there is no point in collecting soldiers if you haven't the remotest idea what to do with them. In August 1914, the British believed that the more men you had the speedier and the more complete the victory would be.

It was an error whose enormity seems comical today, even to a world which knows perfectly well the dimensions of the tragedy embodied in the misunderstanding. What happened to all those fervent

WE SHALL WANT YOU AND MISS YOU.

would-be warriors who, closing the door of the cricket pavilion behind them, blacked their hair and queued up to fight for King and Country? What happened to them was that they fell into the hands of that most frightful of all adversaries, the British War Office, whose occupants, still preoccupied with the lessons of the war-before-the-last, were far too busy checking the respectability of the pedigree of the horses in the cavalry to bother about anything so mundane as kit for the *hoi polloi*. In his history of the war, written with the wisdom of half a century's hindsight, A. J. P. Taylor writes:

Kitchener had expected to get perhaps 100,000 volunteers in the first six months, and maybe 500,000 altogether. This was all, and more than all the existing factories could equip with rifles and uniforms. These modest plans were submerged by a wave of patriotic enthusiasm. 500,000 volunteered in the first month; and the recruitment rate ran at over 100,000 a month for eighteen months thereafter. Altogether, Great Britain raised more than three million volunteers. This vast army was not produced by design; it was thrust on a Government and a War Office which did not know what to do with it . . . There were few camps and little equipment. All through the winter of 1914–15, men lived under canvas, and drilled in civilian clothes with walking sticks instead of rifles . . . It was the beginning of their disenchantment.

What is so fascinating about this attitude of jingo naïveté, and what links it so irrevocably to the extraordinarily incongruous nature of the postcards which circulated in the Great War, is that it perished in one place and flourished concurrently in another. In Flanders its fervent unworldliness was quickly disfigured by shrapnel, gouged by bayonets, raked with machine-gun fire, mashed by shells, trodden underfoot by the marching boots of the infantry, and then left to the rats. But at home no such horrors assailed it. On the contrary, its survival was seen by many of our Betters as utterly necessary to the successful administration of the war; after all, if people were to lose the bloom of their idealism, false idealism though it might be, what then? So it was that while at home genteel ladies thoughtfully distributed white feathers, German measles was regarded as treason, and the mob smashed shop windows for no better reason than that they were too illiterate to pronounce correctly the name over the door, less than a hundred miles to the east, arms and legs, eyes and hands, hearts and genitals were being removed from their owners with a profligate violence which still turns posterity's stomach two generations later. On the first day of the Battle of the Somme, on that long-lost morning when poor Captain Nevill kicked his pathetic football into history, 20,000 British soldiers were killed, and for several days afterwards the vigilant survivors crouching in their trenches were diverted by an unfamiliar sound, the slow diminuendo of the screams of the wounded, left between the lines to savour the sweetness of dying for one's country.

In this context, glance at what was travelling through the mails, back and forth from Britain to the trenches, and wonder at the dichotomy. Seen through the distorting prism of the postcard manufacturers' art, the bloodiest affray in recorded history is transmogrified into a gallant crusade, with the overblown roses of arrant sentimentality garlanding the trench wires, sad ballads of undying love pervading the evening air, seraphic little children waving penny flags in an excess of innocent exhortatory enthusiasm. Saccharine sexuality simpers coyly from the faces of famous home beauties, and the henpeckers of the working classes are seen to be monsters more terrible by far than those to be encountered far away at the Front, in the Man's world. A soldier's uniform is advertised as an aphrodisiac of irresistible potency, and in a series of cards called 'The Patriot', President Poincaré and George V are seen in the company of that indefatigable upholder of Liberty – especially his own – the Czar of Russia. Over the heads of these three oddly assorted gentlemen there flies the banner, 'One Heart, One Mind, One Aim'. And, they might have added, one brain.

The wonderful fatuity of such items must have been underlined at the time by the proximity of the cannon fodder to their nearest and dearest back in England. French newsboys would peddle Northcliffe's dailies in the communication trenches, and, with luck, one of the postcards in this section, dropped hope-

The call of the Flag.

Cheer up
I'll come back
all right

To my dear boy
from Nellie xxxx
I hope the words come True
a hoping to see you soon.

I LOVE MY MOTHERLAND (1).

Motherland! tho' the mighty seas divide us,
   And your sons were scatter'd one and all,
There came a day—your fam'ly were united,
   'Twas the day they heard your call.
Other nations ask the reason why:
From each of us they hear this proud reply.

BAMFORTH COPYRIGHT.   WORDS BY PERMISSION OF THE STAR MUSIC PUBLISHING CO., LONDON.

THE ANCHOR'S WEIGHED (4).

"Go, then," she cried, "but let thy constant
    mind
Oft think of her you leave in tears behind."
"Dear maid, this last embrace my pledge
    shall be,
   The anchor's weigh'd, the anchor's weigh'd,
Farewell! Farewell! Remember me."

BAMFORTH (COPYRIGHT).

TAKE ME BACK TO DEAR OLD BLIGHTY. (2).

Take me back to dear old Blighty, put me on the train —
    for London town,
Take me over there, drop me anywhere,
Birmingham, Leeds, or Manchester—well, I don't care!
I should love to see my best girl, cuddling up again we
    soon shall be;
Whoa! Tiddley-iddley-ighty, hurry me home to Blighty—
    Blighty is the place for me.

BAMFORTH COPYRIGHT   WORDS BY PERMISSION OF THE STAR MUSIC PUBLISHING CO., LONDON

TAKE ME BACK TO DEAR OLD BLIGHTY (3).

One day, Mickey O'Shea, stood in a trench somewhere,
   So brave, having a shave, and trying to part his hair;
Mick yells (dodging the shells and lumps of dynamite):
   Talk of the Crystal Palace on a firework night!

BAMFORTH COPYRIGHT   WORDS BY PERMISSION OF THE STAR MUSIC PUBLISHING CO., LONDON.

JUST BEFORE THE BATTLE, MOTHER (1).

Just before the battle, Mother, I am thinking most of you,
While upon the field we're watching, with the enemy in view.
Comrades brave are round me lying, filled with thoughts of
friends and home,
For well they know that on the morrow some will sleep
beneath the tomb.

BAMFORTH COPYRIGHT.

WHAT DID YOU DO IN THE GREAT WAR, DADDY? (3).

"What is that medal you're wearing, Daddy?
Why is your sleeve empty there?"
A pause and a sigh—then came this reply:
"I gave that for Britain, no need to ask why,
And if my country were calling for men,
Why! I'd do the same, lad, again!"

BAMFORTH COPYRIGHT. BY PERMISSION OF THE LAWRENCE WRIGHT MUSIC CO., DENMARK ST., LONDON, W.

TILL THE SANDS OF THE DESERT GROW COLD (3).

The desert, a burning sea,
A barrier stands 'tween thee and me;
Or love, fast as light, I'd hasten to thee,
Quenching my thirst in thee.
Noon suns find me far beyond the caravan,
Death there warns me how vain is the strength of man.
Love me, I'll love thee.

BAMFORTH COPYRIGHT. WORDS BY PERMISSION OF B. FELDMAN & CO.

KATHLEEN MAVOURNEEN (4)

Mavourneen, Mavourneen, my sad tears are falling
To think that from Erin and thee I must part;
It may be for years and it may be for ever,
Then why art thou silent, thou voice of my heart?
Then why art thou silent, thou voice of my heart?

BAMFORTH COPYRIGHT. WORDS BY PERMISSION OF EVANS & CO.

fully in a letter-box in Surbiton or Southport or Swansea, might reach the soldier only two or three days later. What must the recipients have thought of them? All the resources of irony could hardly have contained their amused contempt, their derisive bawdry. And yet they played the game, sending back messages of the 'hope this finds you in the pink as it leaves me' variety, ostensibly confirming the domestic rumour of those trailing roses and those patriotically pursed rosebud lips, and providing a brilliant example of how documentation can sometimes mislead the historian.

In fact, it is precisely *because* the postcards present an utterly counterfeit impression, of a kind of war which had never really existed, that they remain such vital historical documents; paradoxically, their very falsity reveals a profound truth about the Great War, which was the unbridgeable gulf of comprehension between combatant and non-combatant. The truth of life in the trenches, with the stench of putrescent human flesh mingling with the more refined aroma of clockwork commanders fighting with their backs to the wall of some suitably remote château, never became, or ever could become, real to those who had not lived through it. The euphemism of official war bulletins, which spoke of 'brisk' actions when they meant 50 per cent casualties, kept the level of imagery down to that of a rugby football report in some local country newspaper, while behind the conspiracy there was always the Censor to curb any tendencies to candour on the part of the fighting man. As Lloyd George said, 'the whole thing is horrible, and beyond human nature to bear . . . the correspon-

You'll see I'm getting through alright!

dents don't write, and the censor wouldn't pass, the truth'. It was the Great War more than any event in modern history that split the British into two nations, those who knew the reality of the trenches, and those who could not help imagining it as some kind of super-colossal board game with little coloured flags to mark the advances and retreats of the official communiqués. The breach was never repaired; when the survivors came home they spent the rest of their lives withholding, often even from themselves, the facts of life in the trenches of Flanders. There was, of course, no television to reveal the actuality, but if there had been, it is hardly conceivable that the war would have continued very far into 1917. Lloyd George was convinced that if people only knew what was happening they would countenance it no longer. But they didn't know.

Posterity may wonder why the soldiers never told them. Why was it that instead of writing to their dependents and giving them some idea of what the war was like, they held to the stilted cadences of threepenny etiquette books, with their 'Cheerio, must close now' and 'The cake tasted fine' exit lines? Admittedly there was the censorship in which Lloyd George appears to have had so much faith, but only a half-wit could have failed to find a way of circumventing the moth-eaten blanket of evasion in which the divisional censors attempted to muffle the truth; when Wilfred Owen wished to inform his mother that he had returned to the Front, he would use a double line to cross out certain words. General French's system was even better, but then he was a general, which meant that by the rules of the game he was allowed to write love letters to his mistress in which he chatted about those very troop movements whose disclosure by Other Ranks would have meant a court martial and a firing squad. And even if the censors succeeded in their job, there was always word-of-mouth when the soldiers came home on leave; a man might get his head blown off in the cause of duty, but not even the War Cabinet could arrange to cut his tongue out. Why, then, the total refusal of the soldiers to depart very far from the implications of the cheerful or sentimental postcard? The explanation is unique in the annals of warfare, as indeed was the war itself. The truth was simply too obscene to convey to those who had never experienced it for themselves. With a kind of weary sapience, the trench-fighter, knowing that nothing he could say or

The ironies of history know no bounds. Of the general, Kitchener, and the admiral, Jellicoe, it was Kitchener who died at sea and Jellicoe on land. At the victorious battle of Jutland, Jellicoe sank 62,233 tons of German warships, his own negligible losses amounting to a mere 111,908 tons. With victories like that, who needs disasters?

BRAVE DEFENDERS

We've got the ships and the boys in blue,
We've got the MAN to guide them, too.

MY HEART'S IN MY HOMELAND

My heart's in my homeland, beyond the deep blue sea,
The world's dark and lonely, but glad I shall be
When some day I go to that far homeland shore.
Where the dear ones are waiting to love me once more.

UNTIL WE MEET AGAIN

Until we meet again I'll pray for you, ...
Until the clouds depart, and the skies are blue;
Dark tho' the night may be, love's star will reign,
God keep you true to me, until we meet again.

KEEP THE KETTLE BOILING, MARY

Keep the kettle boiling, Mary, while I'm away,
Don't you fret or worry, Mary, for you I'll pray;
I've got to do my duty far across the foam,
So keep the kettle boiling, dear, till I come marching
home.

THERE'S A SHIP THAT'S BOUND FOR BLIGHTY

There's a ship that's bound for Blighty,
There's a smile behind the tears,
There's a star of hope still shining
Through the dark dark dreary years;
There's a day of joy for someone,
When the night of pain is through.
For the ship that's bound for Blighty
May bring a loved one home to you

CALLING ME HOME TO YOU

There is a heart I love, waiting beyond the foam,
Watching for me and praying, calling me home;
Life that is sweet and fair, love that shall wake anew,
Will they not crown your soul and mine when I
come home to you!

Published by Messrs. Boots & Co. London

SOMEWHERE IN FRANCE, DEAR MOTHER (1).

Out in a trench 'midst the Belgian and French,
A young Irish soldier lay down;
In the midst of the fight took his first chance to write
To his mother in Tipperary Town.
"Bedad," said he, "It must be short,
For they censor ev'ry note";
So to cheer her poor old Irish heart,
Shure! This is what he wrote.

SOMEWHERE IN FRANCE, DEAR MOTHER (2).

Somewhere in France, dear mother, somewhere—but I can't tell,
In the midst of the fray, I'm writing to say that I'm still alive
    and well;
There's some fine big boys from Tipperary, somewhere in
    France with me,
So cheer up, dear, the next time you hear, I'll be somewhere
    in Germany.

SOMEWHERE IN FRANCE, DEAR MOTHER (3).

We now change the scene, for the postman has been,
And outside the old cabin door,
A mother in tears, it's the first time she hears
From her boy who is fighting in the war;
Still full of pride she dries her eyes,
And soon forgets her pain,
She seems to hear him singing
As she reads it once again.

write would do his theme justice, reverted to harmless
cliché.

In order to convey the dimensions of the chasm
which separated the young-old men in Flanders from
the jingo innocents at home, let us recall once more
that well-meant gesture from Dr Grace, a gesture
which implied that in some mysterious way the suffer-
ing of the soldiers in the mud would be rendered
more bearable if they knew that everyone at home was
being made as miserable as officialdom could contrive
to make them. What would Grace and his generation
have made of the flippancy, surely in execrable taste,
of those 'able-bodied' men for whom not even the
horrors of trench warfare could quite eradicate the
recollection of 'pleasure-seeking':

*June 24, 1915: Vermelles. . . . This afternoon we had a
cricket match, officers versus sergeants, in an enclosure
between some houses out of observation of the enemy,
Our front line is perhaps three-quarters of a mile away.
I made top score, 24; the bat was a bit of a rafter, the
ball a piece of rag tied round with string; and the wicket
a parrot cage with the clean, dry corpse of a parrot inside.
It had evidently died of starvation when the French
evacuated the town. Machine-gun fire broke up the
match.*

The soldier so proud of his top score of 24 was
Robert Graves, and the match he records was being
played out even as Dr Grace was dying at the age of
sixty-seven, brought to a premature grave, in the
opinion of Conan Doyle, by the demands on his heart
of a war whose morality he could not comprehend.

If the postcards in this section tell us nothing
about the fighting man at whose sensibilities they were
aimed, they speak volumes when it comes to the civilian and what he thought would be most suitable
under the circumstances. And so patriotism finally
expires with the bathetic gurgle of popular songs
addressed to silver-haired mamas protected from the
inroads of fate by an aureole of white candyfloss; of
professional beauties like Miss Edna May, half-
throttled by a green bonnet-ribbon but still bravely
contriving to look as though butter wouldn't melt, or
Miss Billie Burke, future wife of Florenz Zeigfeld,
standing coyly before the ramparts of a Ruritanian
castle of dreams; of close-ups of Kitchener's droop-
ing moustache. By the time of the second of the wars
to end war, the British had learned honesty with
regard to their postcards; there is a gulf of several
centuries between those chaste ladies in the photographic studios of the Great War and their cartoon
successors of the second war, with breasts exposed and
imaginations kindled by the convenient duality of

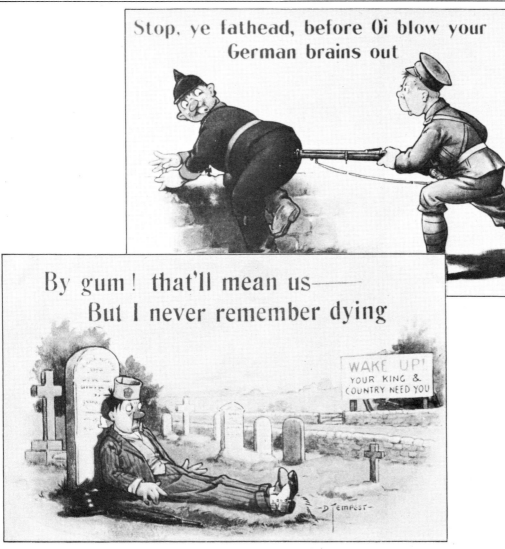

Stop, ye fathead, before Oi blow your German brains out

By gum! that'll mean us—But I never remember dying

WAKE UP! YOUR KING & COUNTRY NEED YOU

meaning attached to the word 'privates'.

There is one other way in which the postcards of the Great War are unlike any others. When we encounter them today, in junk shops or in antique collections, when we stumble on their unmistakable aura of musk and pathos, we rarely bother with the floral scenes of Torquay or the profiles of beauteous ladies or the scenes of smiling soldiers marching off to death and mutilation. For once we ignore the blandishments of the postcard artists and concentrate instead on the messages to their sender. We look closely at the faded, spidery ink, hoping perhaps to find a revelation which will explain the whole business. We never do find it, because no such revelation exists. Instead we find ourselves confronted by bland gratitude for woollen socks, inscrutable thanks for the Christmas cake, and always, the wish that 'this finds you in the pink as it leaves me'. Glancing at the signature, we wonder idly if the poor wretch ever made it back to Blighty. And then we forget about it.

'Having a wonderful time.' A war-time message from Dunkirk and its sender. Lucky in war, he survived

Things are going down A.1. since we started training

Left—Left—Left!
Somewhere a voice is calling.

Well, by gum! the war'll soon be over, now, Bill, if tha's owt to do with it!—I nivver knew thee stop at one job long.

Good-bye, Pat;—and when you meet the Bulgars, knock L out of 'em!

What did your son do in the Army?
I haven't one!
No, when I come to look at yer I should shay sho!

Heavy pressure on all fronts!
—Reuter.

"There's a long, long trail a-trickling!"
And he ought to be ashamed of himself when this lot's through!

Just a line to let you know I'm pegging along alright———— and there's no Hindenburg Line about this, it's unbreakable!

"Blighty!"
No improvement to report on this front!

How do, Fritz!——They say the German Army's a machine: are you one of the nuts?

I hear you're moving—trust the night will be a fine one.

This war bread's hitting some of us pretty hard!

GO HON!
I'm Making Shells.

O memories that bless and burn!

HELP!
where's my respirator?

By gum! I should look soft if a Zeppelin came now.

I always was a loving soul, even with me enemies——but I think Kaiser Bill's muckied his ticket now!

Oh! Anuver recked Zeppelum in the Norf Sea!

Boo—ooh! I've got German Measles.

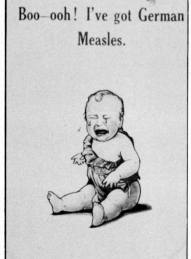

I wish muvver could just get hold of that Kaiser feller—— she'd violate his neutrality!

Loving Thoughts of Dad.

We miss you, Daddy, ever so,
 But you are out to fight the foe;
Oh, we would be brave soldiers, too,
And grow up, Daddy, just like you.

A little Message to Dad.

I'm still a lickle babsy, an' I don't talk
  vewy well,
For my tongue gets all twisted up,—an'
  neiver can I spell;
But Mammie—she be sending dis, to tell
  my gweat big Dad,
I'll be in "knicks" when he comes home,
  and that will make him gwad.

I WANT TO KISS DADDY GOOD-NIGHT.

5
THE FOUR-LETTER WORD

In retrospect the Great War to End Civilisation is seen by those old enough to remember it as something which disturbed, and eventually destroyed, an idyll. This idyll was called the Edwardian Tea Party. It took place in a beautiful garden, and everything in the garden was lovely. The unanimity of this view is striking; reminiscers and memoirists, regardless of social station, see the outbreak of the war as the end of something and the beginning of something else very much worse. In 1964, more than half a century after the event, Sir Compton Mackenzie told me that as the Germans had 'ruined everything', he had resolved never to set foot in Germany as long as he lived. Nor did he. And much lower down the social scale, Frederick Willis, one of the most meticulous recorders of the minutiae of pre-war working-class London life, ends his *Book of London Yesterdays* with a chapter whose title is explained in its opening sentence: 'Nineteen Fourteen is to people of my generation like a Scarlet Line drawn across the story of their lives'. Willis ends that chapter, and his book, as follows:

As the old, familiar world receded into history, we saw our illusions, values, virtues, crumbling away. Even law, order and freedom took on a new look. Youth, the age for love and life, was called upon to die; or much worse, to survive, blind, maimed, shattered in health, or unemployed.

> *Comfort, content, delight –*
> *The age's slow-bought gain –*
> *They shrivelled in a night,*
> *Only ourselves remain.*

That was the end of our sunny stretch of the road.

It may well be that both Mackenzie and Willis, in their starkly differing styles, are merely confusing their own lost innocence with the innocence of the

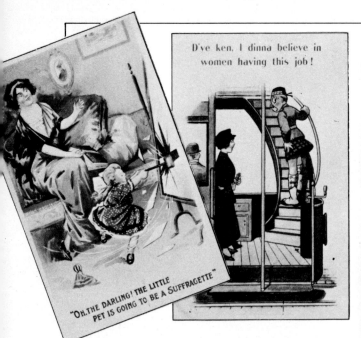

D'ye ken, I dinna believe in women having this job!

"OH, THE DARLING! THE LITTLE PET IS GOING TO BE A SUFFRAGETTE"

Wigan dole queue, 1939

world they remember. But there was indeed a Tea Party going on somewhere, although the likes of Willis never got much closer to its location than to stand on tiptoe and peer over an ivied wall, or to stand waving a penny flag at four horses pulling a closed carriage through City streets. And yet there is a sense in which witnesses like Mackenzie and Willis were justified in seeing the age as a rose-coloured spectacle. For at least that age still carried the frail casket of its own infinite future. It knew nothing of pollution, fall-out, ultimate deterrents, and would have received rumours of the impending death of the planet as a crazy joke in dubious taste. When in 1909 Bernard Shaw put into the mouth of one of his characters the alarming line, 'The writing is on the wall. Rome fell. Babylon fell. Hindhead's turn will come', people smiled and put it down to Irish perversity. Willis depicts the archetypal Londoner as a creature

as happy as we poor mortals can hope to be. Provided he managed to pay his rent he was as safe in his little house as William the First in his Tower of London. Probably he was much safer, and I suspect he loved his little castle much more than William loved his great one.

In the light of this brand of nostalgia, it is understandable enough that we should discover so much anger, sadness and bitterness at the abrupt ending of a genial epoch. But it was not as genial as all that, and it would be a mistake for any of us to think it was. For the Great War, so far from disrupting an idyll, might just as easily be said to have diverted one catastrophe by bringing about another, and it is Willis of all apologists who provides the clue. In that curious little quatrain with which he ends his recollections of the good old days, he implies that in pre-war days the blight of unemployment was unknown. Why, then, that qualification about the Englishman's home being his castle 'provided he managed to pay his rent'? Elsewhere Willis concedes that as far as his lost Londoner was concerned:

security to him was unknown. Of course I mean economic

security, for he had any amount of physical security, since London was the safest city in the world. He took his ease in hundreds of obscure little taverns on Saturday night, and he did not suffer from inhibitions, complexes and frustrations, so was a headache to nobody.

But a man without economic security is bound to be a headache to somebody eventually, even if only to himself, and it would appear that Willis's golden age was much corroded by the acid of political contention, as people massed into armies prepared to fight for the right to procure money, or the right to work, as it is often erroneously defined by sentimental propagandists who never do any themselves. The corrective to the Willis view is provided by a most remarkable

UNEMPLOYMENT?
HERE'S THE REMEDY!

RUSHEM SALTS

WURKEM LIVER SALTS

PILLS
REECHAM

SETTLE ITS POWDER

GETS EM SALTS

ironist called George Dangerfield who, one day in 1935, looked down the lengthening perspectives of history to Willis's dream-world, expecting to find

a nation more or less dancing its way into war, to a sound of lawnmowers and ragtime, to the hum of bees and the popping of champagne corks. But it wouldn't have been true. For as soon as one begins to look into the subject one is confronted with a far more curious drama.

The far more curious drama in question was the impending dissolution of Great Britain, pulled to pieces by the militant Irish, the militant Suffragettes, and above all the militant Unions. As the implications of the shooting at Sarajevo gradually sank into the learned brain of Sir Edward Grey never to be seen

again, the unions were massing for a General Strike, before which, in Dangerfield's words, 'that tired General Strike of 1926 pales into insignificance'.

The issue was Work, its availability, the conditions attached to it, the rewards given for it. Every one of the men and some of the women who smile or smirk out at us from the sanctity of the saucy postcard were obliged to work or starve. The complacent geniality of their laughter, their blissful preoccupation with the affairs of the flesh, belie the desperate urgency of their predicament. Those puritans who disapproved of the salaciousness or the suggestiveness of the cards no doubt overlooked the fact that making love was, and still remains, almost the only pleasure requiring for

67

My word! if I catch you bending.

"THERE'S ONE OF THE GENTLEMEN IN, MA'AM—
I CAN SEE HIS BALD HEAD!"
"GOOD HEAVENS, WOMAN! YOU HAVEN'T A
BALD-HEADED MAN STAYING HERE!"

HE'S STANDING UP NOW—
BLIMEY, WHAT A PHYSIQUE
HE'S GOT!

its indulgence no capital outlay, and was therefore bound to retain its popularity among those for whom the choice was as stark as any choice can be: Work or Starve. The postcard artists preferred to work, and produced a long succession of archetypes – the ominous tread of the policeman, the voyeurism of the window-cleaner, the eye to the main chance of the milkman and the travelling salesman, the valiant adherence to rules and regulations of harassed bus conductors and put-upon counterhands. They all appear to be enjoying themselves mightily. But Dangerfield examined them more closely and discovered that, for instance, in July 1914

There were disputes in the London building trade and in the electrical industry. The Marine Engineers' Union was in a state of ferment. The shipbuilding and engineering trades were demanding an eight-hour day. The engineers and boilermakers were engaged in a complicated battle with the Great Western Railway. The General Labourers' Union was moving for shorter hours, increased wages, and improved conditions. And on July 4 the munition workers of Woolwich Arsenal downed tools.

In a sense the most remarkable thing of all about

Dangerfield's remarkable portrait of industrial England is the fact that it is after all unremarkable. If there was industrial ferment on the eve of the Great War, there always had been industrial ferment, and there always has been ever since. Moreover, there always will be, until some government becomes as wise as its subjects and learns to acknowledge one scandalous truth about work, which none has so far acted upon, but which creeps occasionally into the world of the vulgar postcard. It is a very simple proposition, and its truth is glaringly apparent no matter where the eye falls. But for all that, it seems to have been either overlooked or ignored by the theorists of the modern age. The proposition is this: most people, given the choice, would rather not do any work at all.

Who can blame them? The heroes and heroines of the postcards may be glimpsed *at* their work, dressed *for* their work, but almost none of them are actually seen to be *doing* it. With the worldly wisdom of the townee, they have seen through the sham of the puritan work-ethic and are reacting accordingly. Apart from the publicans and barmaids, who preside over the great bacchanalia, and the policemen, who do what they can to keep it within limits, apart from the bus drivers who carry the drunks home and the conductors who sell them a ticket for the privilege, and apart of course from the doctors and nurses who prod their victims' bodies and the vicars who go through the motions of prodding their souls, the labourers of the postcards use their occupation as the pretext for doing nothing at all, for mucking about, for slipping through the net. That is why there are no postcards raising a laugh at the expense of miners at the coal-face, or of match-workers permitted by a charitable employer to take home free samples of Phossy Jaw. The work situations in the comic postcards have to be those situations where slap-and-tickle is at least possible in theory.

Immeasurable quantities of hypocrisy and hot air have been expended over the years on this issue of work, to say nothing of vast quantities of stupidity

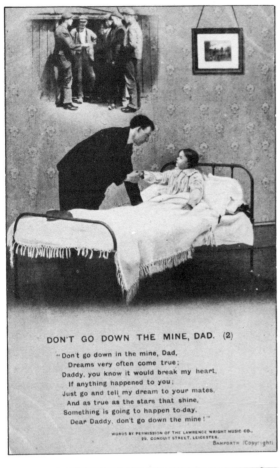

DON'T GO DOWN THE MINE, DAD. (2)

"Don't go down in the mine, Dad,
   Dreams very often come true;
Daddy, you know it would break my heart,
   If anything happened to you;
Just go and tell my dream to your mates,
   And as true as the stars that shine,
Something is going to happen to-day,
   Dear Daddy, don't go down the mine!"

WORDS BY PERMISSION OF THE LAWRENCE WRIGHT MUSIC CO.,
29, CONDUIT STREET, LEICESTER.
BANFORTH (Copyright).

"Wot are you chaps on strike for?"
"Shorter hours."
"Ah! I've allus said that sixty minutes is too long!"

Owing to the increased cost
of living we are having to
economise.

AH, HERE COMES OUR NEW VICAR,
GOOD MORNING!

and evasion. Long before the idea of the Great War was even considered, a movement arose to give the working man something called the Ten-Hour Day, an obscenity whose only justification was that it could at least be said to be an improvement on the even fouler obscenity it was meant to supersede, the Twelve-Hour Day. There was much opposition to the Ten-Hour Day, although curiously enough none at all from the poor wretches who would have to work it. Later in the nineteenth century, there was a like move towards something called the Eight-Hour Day. Lord Salisbury, three times Prime Minister of England, announced that the British working man was 'not ready' for the Eight-Hour Day. Certainly Lord Salisbury was not ready for it, but more diverting even than the crassness of his announcement is its implication, by no means exclusive to his lordship, that the condition of not working, or leisure as a later age describes it, or being alive, as most workers would conceive it, is something mysterious and nebulous towards which the working man has to be educated very gradually.

The idea is so palpably untrue as to be laughable. The British working man has shown a magnificent adaptability to the idea of spending less time working and proportionately more enjoying himself. And why should he not? Only a congenital imbecile would pretend that presiding over the destiny of screws on an endless belt is a more desirable or virtuous way of approaching the grave than chasing pairs of jiggling breasts across the shingle, or that disappearing in the daylight hours down a pit-shaft is a more improving exercise than playing tennis with a young lady uncertain as to how many sizes too small she should be wearing her shorts this season. There never was any particular virtue in work for its own sake, certainly not in the exclusively urban, industrialised world populated by the characters in the comic postcards. It is interesting that in not one single card are we shown a leader of the nation exhorting the masses to

EXCUSE ME — I WAS TOLD TO
ASK FOR THE FOREMAN,
A 'MR. BIGHEAD!

"WHAT ARE YOUR INITIALS?"
"W.C., MISTER!"
"WELL THEY'RE A ROUGH LOT HERE LAD
DON'T LET 'EM SIT ON YOU!"

SAY, PAT, LAD...IF THE BUZZER GOES,
LET GO, WON'T YOU!

The working man soon learns that the most arduous work of all is finding ways of not working. Contrary to the beliefs of successive Prime Ministers, not working is always a great pleasure

THEY SAY <u>FORTY</u> IS A CRITICAL TIME IN A MAN'S LIFE.
WELL, I SHOULD SAY <u>FIVE TO TEN</u> IS MUCH WORSE!

"WHAT SORT OF A JOB WOULD YER HAVE IF YER COULD CHOOSE?"
"DUNNO—BUT LAST TIME I PLAYED DOMINOES, IT STRUCK ME WHAT
A GRAND JOB PAINTING SPOTS ON DOUBLE BLANKS WOULD BE!"

work harder to save everything; nor, for that matter, are we shown the chorus of raspberries with which such appeals are invariably greeted. What we get instead is something much more realistic, very much closer to home, the stock joke of the office boy whose grandmother has the invaluable asset of pegging out not once but several times, and whose last rites always fall on the occasion of a big football match. That office boy and his phoenix of a grandmother represent the sad but true fact that people generally work because they have to, and not, as so many economists and historians seem to believe, because they want to.

The postcard comedians were not quite the only ones to see the joke and capitalise on it. More important than the 'right to work' was, and is, the right to have enough time and money to do something else also. 'Work', said Oscar Wilde, 'is the curse of the drinking classes.' 'Work', said that perpetrator of unspeakable evangelical propaganda Jerome K. Jerome, 'fascinates me. I can sit and look at it for hours. I love to keep it by me; the idea of getting rid of it nearly breaks my heart.' Both Wilde and Jerome, and all the other comedians who treated the Work theme, even down to the artists and caption writers of the vulgar postcards, were dancing with a kind of desperate laughter on the rim of the abyss which had been pointed out to them years before. The news of this abyss had come to English society in the form of a conundrum, and the fact that the gentleman who framed it happened to be a screwball should not detract from the vital importance of his riddle. In 1865 John Ruskin published a book called *Sesame and Lilies*, whose title nobody could understand, because it didn't mean anything. However, it was in *Sesame and Lilies* that Ruskin asked the great Sixty-Four-Thousand-Dollar Question of the nineteenth century: *Which of us is to do the hard and dirty work for the rest, and for what pay? Who is to do the pleasant and clean work, and for what pay?*

The riddle has stood now for more than a century, and still no statesman or philosopher or economist or mystic has managed to answer it to anyone else's satisfaction; very few have even tried. In the meantime, so long as the solution to Ruskin's damnable conundrum remains in abeyance, it is perfectly understandable that everyone who has the opportunity will answer it for himself and behave accordingly. The postcard heroes and heroines, like the heroes and heroines of the mass of the British population, have done everything humanly possible in the way of rectifying the oversights of the law by reducing their Eight-Hour Day as much as they possibly can, conserving their energies for the far more interesting and rewarding demands of sport and recreation. Their ingenuity in this regard may be regrettable; it may even be disastrous, but that does not make it any the less true, or the less understandable. The persistence with which people have put their minds to this problem of reducing their own working time in favour of their own playing time has led some to blame them for the decline and fall of the British Empire. If only everyone had worked a little harder, say these armchair labourers, these horny-handed sons of vicarious toil, then the map of the world might still be pink. As a matter of fact, there is one very important sense in which it still is pink, thanks to the tireless ingenuity of the loafers, the skivers, the overgrown schoolboys.

A PENN'ORTH OF THEM TOWN COUNCILLORS, PLEASE!

WAITER: "WOULD YOU LIKE TONGUE, SIR?"
CUSTOMER: "NO, I NEVER EAT ANYTHING FROM AN ANIMAL'S MOUTH!"
WAITER: "WHAT ABOUT TWO BOILED EGGS, SIR?"

I ONLY WANTED A LITTLE PIECE TO STAND THE TEAPOT ON!

THERE'S A GENTLEMAN COMING IN FOR A WREATH, GLADYS!

HE'S A GENTLEMAN FARMER---HE RAISES NOTHING BUT HIS HAT!

"WHY DID YOU GIVE HIM A DOSE OF THAT, YOU FOOL?"
"HE CAME IN, SIR, AND ASKED FOR SOMETHING TO STOP HIM
COUGHING---AND NOW HE DAREN'T COUGH TO SAVE HIS LIFE!"

"I'M AFRAID YOUR HUSBAND WILL NEVER WORK AGAIN!"
"I'LL GO UPSTAIRS AND TELL HIM DOCTOR—
IT WON'T HALF BUCK HIM UP!"

"HOW IS THE **WIND** I WAS TREATING YOU FOR
LAST YEAR MRS. SIMS?"
"THIS IS IT—IN THE PRAM—DOCTOR!"

"SURE DOCTOR—MY HEART'S IN DEAR OLD **IRELAND!"**
"WELL MURPHY, GET YOUR BOWELS IN THE **FREE STATE**
AND YOU'LL BE ALRIGHT!"

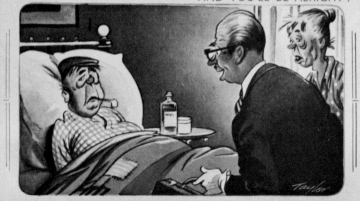

Doctors very soon discover that the Hippocratic oath is by no means the last oath they will ever breathe. Exposure to a populace exclusively preoccupied with bowels, breasts and babies would make even a Pasteur seriously consider vetinerary surgery as an alternative profession

6
NEW BALLS PLEASE

Most historians and politicians, regardless of their nationality or the size of the axe they happen to be grinding, agree that when the British set out to colonise the earth, they failed. Most historians and politicians, however, are quite wrong. Even the British themselves, woefully buried up to the waist in the detritus of a vanished empire, are wrong. No doubt the reason for the misconception has much to do with the fact that those scholars who rewrite the events of the past, and those administrators who pretend to adjust the events of the future, tend as groups to be muscle-bound to the point of paralysis. Having made the catastrophic mistake of correlating play with childhood, they have proceeded with the serious business of life and by so doing have overlooked the one achievement of the empire-builders which has indeed turned out to be enduring. It is an achievement which has conquered so large a propor-

tion of the earth that in the mid-1970s, barely a century after the great campaign got under way, it has become very nearly impossible to nominate any political unit in the world which has remained impervious to the great British revelation.

In a sense the very vastness of the triumph has obscured its nature, for its effects have become so ingrained a part of daily life, from China to Chile, from Lagos to Leipzig, that nobody stops to wonder any more what life was like before the change took place. Then again there is the ridiculous propaganda of the theorists to obscure the issue still further – Herbert Spencer, for instance, whose announcement that 'a proficiency at billiards is a sign of an ill-spent youth' was one of the great philosophic blunders of the nineteenth century; and Kipling, whose silly squeaks about the muddied oaf and the flannelled fool are, in their own comic way, beautifully charac-

BILLIARD EXPRESSIONS.

A GOOD BREAK.

BILLIARD EXPRESSIONS.

PUTTING ON SIDE.

BILLIARD EXPRESSIONS.

A KISS OFF THE CUSHION.

teristic of a man who was probably more deficient in a sense of fair play than any other great writer of his time. And yet, Spencer and Kipling notwithstanding, were we to place the contents of this next group of postcards before an average male born in, say, 1790, it is doubtful if he would react to a single nuance of the humour, or even be able to grasp what it was that the people in the illustrations were supposed to be doing or what the practical application was of the curious implements they were brandishing. His bewilderment would be augmented by the amusement of his grandson, who would glance at the cards and laugh at all those points where the artist would expect him to laugh, in just the same way that, while Tom Jones at Dingly Dell is unthinkable, Pickwick's presence there is one of the great truisms of the English experience. For between Fielding and Dickens there occurred a great social revolution, and the fact that most history books ignore it does not lessen its significance.

The nature of this revolution is most succinctly defined by an outstanding exception among historians, Sir Robert Ensor, who, in his *Oxford History of England, 1870–1914*, states that

. . . the development of organised games, which, on any reckoning may rank among England's leading contributions to world-culture, has been far more recent than is often realised.

Sir Robert then provides a list of dates to support his argument, but before we come to them it is important to list the first date of all, 1861. In that year, the Clarendon Commission was formed at the request of Palmerston and instructed to look into the nature of the education being received by the upper classes. The outcome was the Public Schools Act of 1869, which effected the institutionalisation not only of studies but also of leisure. For the first time in history, the development of 'manly sports' became a national policy, although by the time Establishment rumps were seated at the table of the Clarendon Commission, the process was already under way. The first Open Golf Championship was held in 1860; the Football Association was formed in 1863 and the Rugby Union in 1871. Two years later Lawn Tennis was invented and the County Cricket Championship

took its traditional shape. 1880 saw the formation of the Amateur Athletic Association, followed four years later by the Amateur Boxing Association and the year after that by the Billiard Association.

English life was utterly transformed, and the instrument of its transformation was the most influential export ever shipped out by one nation for the curiosity of another. In every instance the process of percolation was identical. The questing minds and excess energy of young patricians combined to create a new way of wasting time. This new process was codified and formalised, and spread, via the great Public Schools, through the ranks of the middle classes and eventually to the Great Unwashed. Concurrently the empire-builders, taking with them overseas the accoutrements of the life they enjoyed, the camp baths and the shoe-trees, the shirt-studs and the sauce-boats, the soda siphons and the collapsible writing-desks, took also their stumps and rackets, their oars and cues. They demonstrated the use of these bizarre weapons in the imperial crusade to millions of natives who began by gawping blankly and ended by executing the late cut and the forehand smash with such muscular expertise that a hundred years later the English found themselves unable to win any international trophies for the very team games they had invented.

Perhaps, of all those games, the genesis of Snooker is most instructive as to how the operation worked. Indeed, the case history of Snooker is so archetypal that it reads very much like a parody of Kipling's *Plain Tales From the Hills*. In 1875, at the hill station of Ootacamund in southern India, a subaltern with the appeasing name of Neville Chamberlain was pottering in the club, at the billiard table. Quickly becoming disenchanted with the permutations of the three balls, two white and one coloured, he suddenly had the idea of adding to them a fourth ball, also coloured, and soon saw that he had stumbled upon the possibilities of a new game. Soon the rules and procedure of this game were hammered out and a copy of them hung on the club wall, where they began what James Morris in *Pax Britannica* calls 'their phenomenal journey around the world'. There was one other problem which young Chamberlain solved,

England's most influential export. W.G. Grace sits
third from left

and that was the question of a name for the game he
had invented. In the end he decided to call it after the
term then in use in the army in India to denote a
first-year officer cadet; the term was a 'snooker'.

The speed with which the new gospel of team
games grasped the world's imagination can be gauged
with mathematical precision simply by studying the
results of international contests involving the British,
the masters, and the foreigners, their pupils. We find
that in the first three international football matches
played between the professionals of England and
Austria in Vienna in 1908–9 the visitors won every
time, with a goal average of 25 to Austria's 3, and that
the fourth game played between the two sides, again
in Vienna, in 1930, resulted in a goalless draw. At
Wimbledon, between the institution of the Men's
Singles in 1877 and the outbreak of the Great War,
the British and the Australians shared the trophy between them. From 1919 to the present time, only one
Englishman, Fred Perry, has been successful. Between

1900 and 1914, only one foreigner, a Frenchman,
succeeded in winning the Open Golf Championship.
In 1900 at Bristol the West Indies' touring cricket
side was afforded only second-class status, and was
reduced to such impotence by the Gloucestershire
batsman Jessop that the visiting bowlers lay down in
the grass and laughed at their own ineptitude; fifty
years later a team from the same islands made a
mockery of English Test-batting techniques. And so
on. Through the twentieth century Jack has proved
to be as good as, and eventually better than, his
master. But nowhere has the idea of team games as
recreation taken hold of the mass consciousness more
firmly than in Britain, and the salacious, suggestive,
vulgar, crude, coarse funny postcard inevitably an-
nexed the sporting territory as part of its own
empire.

In effect the arrival of sport and games into the
world of the comic postcard proved a most valuable
one for those professional punners and purveyors of
double entendre who provided the postcard world with
its creative material. For one of the inescapable facts
of life about almost all team games is that they involve
items of equipment called balls; and the moment
balls come into their own, so does the gift for bawdry
of the English common man. Some balls are much
larger than others, as Dr Grace discovered when, in
old age, he forsook cricket for the more contemplative
delights of bowls. Then again, some balls are much
harder than others, as every schoolboy discovers on
the day he graduates from underarms with a tennis
ball to overarms with a composition ball. The male
golfer playing a mixed foursome who announces the

I SHOULD SO MUCH LIKE TO BE WITH YOU.

A GOOD CATCH IN THE LONG FIELD.

I'M MAKING A HIT AMONG THE GIRLS!

I'VE CAUGHT A FINE "FLAPPER" HERE!

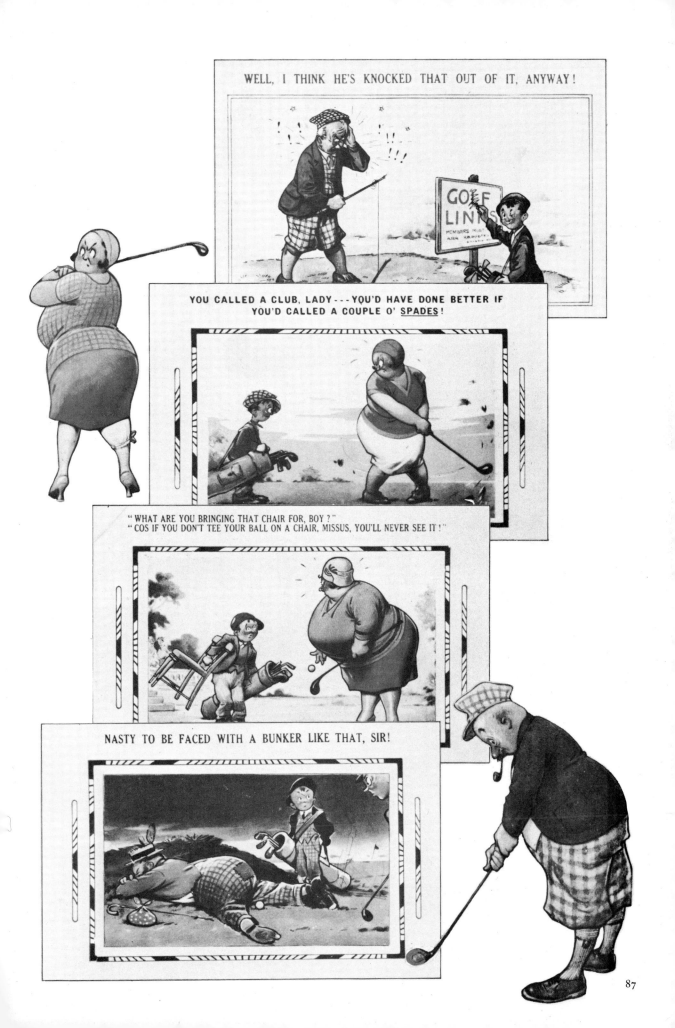

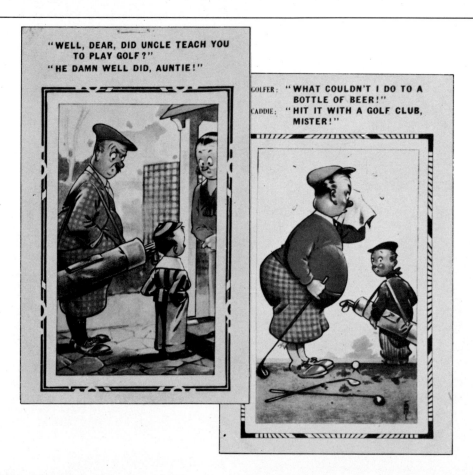

loss of his balls may not always find his predicament taken with the degree of gravity he would wish, and if he happens to explain to somebody who has led a sheltered life that the object of the game is to roll the balls into the hole, his social life might easily find itself coming to an abrupt halt. The caption writers of the emergent days of the popularisation of ball games must have positively salivated when all these possibilities dawned upon them. A whole new area in which to exploit their grubby ingenuities. Who, one wonders, was the first hack to jump at the news that in cricket it is well within the bounds of possibility to bowl a maiden over without stepping within a thousand yards of the female of the species; that it is easy to be six feet five inches tall and still have two short legs; that conceivably Dracula, had he attended Charterhouse or Radley and aspired to a place in the first eleven, might well have cherished a school report saying, 'A poor bowler and slovenly field, but shows great promise as a bat'.

The other sports have been no less generous in their contributions to the cause of the dirty laugh. The joke about pocket billiards, for example, is no more nor less than a dry-land equivalent of the bathing joke about what we have we hold, while many a scriptwriter has drawn on the idea that a man will never go around with a woman unless he is sure he can go three rounds with her husband. Tennis-watching cats who murmur, 'My brother's in that racket', campers who innocently inquire of each other where they are hanging out at the moment, fishermen who dally in the long reeds with the local siren and are

then asked if they have ever caught anything, all these jokes are born of the questing spirit which once inspired young Chamberlain to increase the number of his balls, if one may be pardoned for putting it that way. But then, how else is one to put it?

The other great asset which the province of the comic postcard acquired when team games revolutionised English life was the fact that, when young ladies aspire to technical expertise in even the most sedentary of sports, certain sections of their anatomies tend to protrude, just as they do when riding a bicycle or hiking in short shorts. It was Oscar Wilde who induced apoplexy among the patricians at Lord's when he observed that he found cricket offensive because 'the batting posture was indecent'. What he would have made of young ladies who attempt to bat we shall never know, but since sport has become bisexual, most of the postures are, if not indecent, highly provocative. There is many a front-row forward languishing in a public house somewhere at this very moment dreaming the same old dream of scrumming down with eight forwards from a ladies' fifteen. And as for the Chamberlain brigade, many of that company are past masters at handing the cue to a lady and then standing back to observe not the straightness of the cue but the curvaceousness of the player holding it. One fondly recalls the dirty jokes of one's schooldays, about the goalkeeper's daughter who . . . but this is hardly the place for such irreverent reflections. Comic postcards are a serious business, and the playing of games a positively solemn one, at least so far as the English are concerned.

7
ABREAST OF FASHION

There was one other game, more popular than any of the rest, and with far more venerable antecedents than any of those approved by Arnold of Rugby. It was, and still is, regarded as a ladies' game, and certainly most women in most epochs have played it with a ruthless if instinctive professionalism at some moment in their lives. But so have a great many men, and if the attention in the postcard world seems for the most part to be drawn towards the lady players, that is only because the artists were men, directing their work at a predominantly male audience. The game in question was dressing-up, making-up, being in the style, looking 'nice', giving members of the opposite sex something to think about by being alluring, and members of your own a nasty smack in the eye by being more up to the minute than they were.

Since saucy postcards first began appearing in newsagents' and confectioners' shops, the rules as to what is and is not permissible have constantly been amended, as the student notices the moment he starts comparing items from successive decades. And one thing he is quick to perceive is that if some aspects of the social scene in the last hundred years describe a more tortuous pattern than others, perhaps Dress is the least complicated of all. The evolutionary pattern of fashion in clothes in the period between Victoria and her great-great-granddaughter describes a straight line, from camouflage to candour, protection to exposure, evasion to disclosure, from more clothes to less. Obviously this progress has been of vital interest to the postcard artist, obliged to sail as close to the winds of nudity as he can without running foul of Watch Committees and the police courts. As the British were released from the bonds of sexual reticence by two great acts of liberation – from fear of Jehovah by

"That's a nice shape, Henry."
"Yes, dear; I admire it very much."

if it ever occurred to Tempest, Taylor and company as they brought those upper and nether millstones of popular morality, the neckline and the hemline, closer and ever closer together that they were pushing on, almost despite themselves, towards the last frontier of the Altogether. And did they, like their detractors, equate this ultimate in undress with the ultimate in salaciousness? If they did, then they were very much mistaken, for the modern age has nothing much more prurient to offer than the wasp-waisted freaks of Edwardian high life.

The Victorians had of course developed the technique of apparently accidental *décolletage* to a fine and highly revealing art, but in the line illustrations of the period the Victorian was not really a person at all, so much as a bundle of clothes with a head sticking out of the top. In any case there is something deeply suspect about an age which could take the ancient idea of the suggestively protuberant female bottom and develop it as the institution of the bustle was developed in mid-century. As for the crinoline, which for a while, say from 1860 to 1870, superseded the bustle, there is a drawing by John Leech entitled 'Dressing for the Ball in 1857' which renders the idea of nakedness positively virginal by comparison. A slender young girl, assisted by four maids, is in the process of being surrounded by a large cage which has been designed for the express purpose of concealing utterly the line of the wearer's waist, hips and bottom, thereby making the men who meet her think of nothing else. The Empress Eugénie employed one lady-in-waiting who testified that in the heyday of the crinoline 'it was almost impossible for three ladies to sit together in one small room'. And the curiously arthritic characters in Leech's drawings bear witness to the conspiracy. The dull young things in his illustrations, as they drift about the garden with a Trollopean desultory air, tapping croquet balls through the same hoops which one day soon their

Darwin and from fear of endless children by the availability of cheap methods of birth control – they began to unwrap themselves from the miles of cloth and lace and silk and cotton in which they had been mummified for much of the nineteenth century. The postcard artists kept abreast of, and perhaps a shade ahead of, the movement. One cannot help wondering

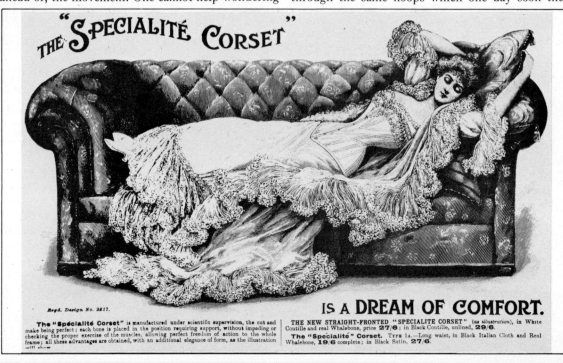

husbands will be jumping through, are stiffened into peculiarly Anglo-Saxon attitudes by buckram and horsehair and whalebone to the point where we begin to wonder how any act of seduction ever took place at all without the assistance of an army of retainers.

It was the Edwardians, ever practical and business-like when it came to hedonistic pursuits, who simplified matters. In the great swirling confusion of practical inventions which characterised the Edwardian age, none was more significant than the disappearance of underwear in favour of something naughtily Parisian called Lingerie. When the Bamforths first began stumbling towards their concept of the mass-produced postcard, feminine underwear was still being marketed on the hypocritical but polite assumption that it was something which nobody apart from the wearer ever actually set eyes on. But with the Edwardians, a lady's under-garments were transformed from artefacts to keep her warm under the dress to devices to keep men hot under the collar. When underwear was superseded by lingerie the assumption was perfectly clear. The man would eventually gaze upon the woman undressed. Naturally what he saw must be designed to inflame him still further with desire. So flannel drawers were replaced by knickers, the shift by the slip, the petticoat by articles known to the trade as frillies. The passing thought occurs that, as inventions like the crinoline, which required countless yards of material, had been popularised so that dressmakers and haberdashers could grow fat on the proceeds, this progress from swathing armour to scanty exposure might have drastically reduced the margin of profit among the couturiers. That this was not so is due to a curious truth about the fashion-conscious, whatever their sex; the less material required, the more they can be gulled into paying for it. Before the Edwardian age was over, the pretty little noodles of society were paying up to £50 for a petticoat – at a time when the maids who were helping them into and out of their underwear were earning £15 a year.

If silhouettes seem to become a little more pointed around the start of the Great War, it is because in 1912 the Edwardians launched the ultimate weapon in the war of titillation, the Brassière. By that time the mashers and the knuts (usually spelt as 'nuts' by the postcard caption writers) were passing away, and their position was being usurped by a fresh generation of young men delighted to discover that as the years went by, there appeared to be less and less yardage to get through before arriving at the real thing. Even so, when we gaze now at those projections of canoodling Edwardian plebs, what we are observing is not the Homeric encounter of flesh upon flesh, but only its Tennysonian variant, cambric clashing against blue serge, or flannel caressing bombasine, a comedy of sartorial manners which calls to mind that unfortunate adolescent eponymous hero of Booth

NUT GATHERER.

TOO MUCH & TOO LITTLE.

"A "NUT" WITH A SMALL SCREW."

"I'VE CAUGHT ON HERE ALRIGHT."

Tarkington's *Seventeen* who finally manoeuvres the girl of his dreams on to his knee, only to find himself hopelessly inhibited by the fact that the trousers on which the young lady is reclining are a pair of his father's hand-me-downs.

The fact that in the Victorian era ladies had been required to present themselves to the outside world as legless contraptions which moved by some for-

The 'nut' is a fop, or a dude, a young man wise enough to know that the most interesting object apart from himself is a young woman

GREEN NUTS

COCOA NUTS

tuitous clockwork arrangement demanding no apparent movements at all below the thighs, does not necessarily mean that prudery was fashion's sole arbiter. There was also the important consideration of keeping warm, if not from the waist up then at least from the knees down. And it was not only the loosening of moral restraints which, inch by inch, sanctioned the gradual unveiling of the female form, but also the daft impracticality of the old-style cocooning. John Leech's twittering young miss, who could not be wheeled out to her first ball without the backstage connivance of a whole army of domestic workers, would have taken one anguished glance at new inventions like the bicycle, and have known that so far as her own social survival was concerned it was a question of stripping down or fading away. And what a relief for the girls of the post-war enlightenment to know that no longer would they be obliged to lift the skirt-hem above the horse-dung when crossing the filthy streets of some great city. Furthermore, if the ladies were serious about extending the limits of their freedom, clearly something would have to be done about all that hair. Ronald Pearsall, in his study of Edwardian social life, reminds us about the grand society ladies:

A great deal of time was spent in having their hair done. Extravagant coiffures were built up on pads and with the aid of wire frames. Consequently tall women looked grotesque and short women top-heavy. The ideal woman was shaped like a swan, but crowned with their outrageous hats many ladies gave the impression of being

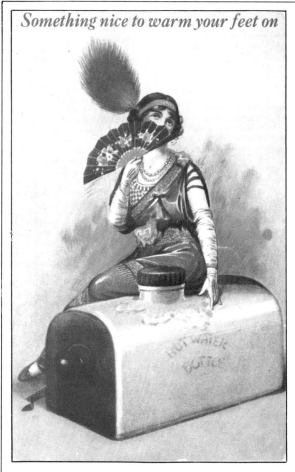

Something nice to warm your feet on

I've got a nice little handful here

dolls that had been put together in an odd sort of way.
So indeed were the hats themselves, which often incorporated the trappings of dead birds, facsimiles of fruit salads, or miniatures of the Botanical Gardens in Regent's Park. (In an early episode of television's celebration of Edwardiana, *Upstairs, Downstairs*, located *circa* 1908, the footman, about to leave for the church to attend a family wedding, demonstrates one of the most beloved of all working-class *double entendre* when he glances at the scullery maid's hat and declares that if he should get hungry during the ceremony he can always take a bite of her cherries.)

It seems that when it came to a girl's hat, literally anything went; the finished article was, certainly in working-class circles, the receptacle for every stray item of haberdashery or horticulture in the house, a crazy gallimaufry of rejects and discoveries, bits and pieces, unconsidered trifles which the female Autolycus had been shrewd enough to snap up with an eye for the future. Here is Jenny, the milliner-heroine of Frank Swinnerton's *Nocturne* (1917), having a busman's holiday one winter night after supper, gathering the raw material for yet another glorious episode in the history of creative hat-making:

The box proved to contain a large number of 'bits' of all sizes and kinds – fragments of silk (plain and ribbed), of plush, of ribbon, both wide and narrow; small sprays of marguerites, a rose or two, some poppies and a bunch of violets; a few made bows in velvet and silk; some elastic, some satin, some feathers, a wing here and there.

The constructions which emerged from this arcane

empirical science naturally required large hatpins to keep them in place, which means that with the eventual passing of what one might call the flora-and-fauna school of millinery, there passed also the last legitimate excuse for a girl to carry on her person a lethal weapon for repelling unwelcome boarders; in at least one Hollywood melodrama of the 1930s, a male lecher goes to his makers when the heroine, undesirous of his attentions, gives him a sharp jab in the libido with her hatpin.

AFTER A FASHION.

LUCKY DOG.

Those alarming reveries were recorded by the novelist J. B. Priestley, who, having been born in the provinces in 1894, was at precisely the right stage of adolescent yearning to savour vicariously the best – and the worst – of organised Edwardian prurience. Priestley makes another point in favour of exposure in the cause of morality when he says that the short skirts of the 1920s were a tremendous source of disillusionment to young men because they revealed the imperfections of what had once only been imagined.

The same process has been taking place ever since. As the two-piece bathing suit scandalised those whose prime had happened to coincide with the one-piece bathing suit, so the bikini outraged supporters of the more conventional two-piece suit. When hemlines plummeted through the machinations of Yves St Laurent in 1947, winning the title 'The New Look' for what was really a very old, not to say an ancient look, there were many men who actually found the process of thigh-and-calf concealment stimulating. If they were telling the truth about that, then their hour of glory was brief indeed, for not very far into the future lay that deadly device for separating the female dogs from the dolls, the mini-skirt. Finally there was the topless outfit, that peculiarly elusive phenomenon which, in the experience of most men, is popular in the next town but never in their own.

In the face of this kind of hysterical emancipation, what was left for the postcard artists to be suggestive about? Their policy has always been to draw the female form in the kind of erect position which would require all the whalebone and horsehair of the Victorians, but with almost no clothes on at all. Those blushing contemporary beauties with the rampant

I'M THINKING OF YOU ALL THE TIME

What was the effect of all this subterfuge and upholstery and boosting of parts, this camouflaging and highlighting and tactical exposure of the body? No doubt it was very much more erotic and frustrating to the male than anything to be found in a saucy postcard. In fact, the effect on the young adoring Edwardian male could be positively alarming. One glance at those tortuously constricted waists, those mounds of bosom bubbling up like animated balloons, those stiff hobbled walks and those protruding behinds, and the virginal male was immediately inflamed by nightmare visions of giantesque amazons descending on him in a great amorphous mass of sexuality:

So the illicit affair, however dangerous, the little tap on the bedroom door behind which the delicious creature, with heroic bared bosom and those great marmoreal thighs, was waiting – oh it was all irresistible. Such longings, such imaginings, such thoughts, charged the very air with sexuality.

WE HAVE TO KEEP PACE WITH
THE TIMES, OH YEAH!
WE HAVE TO KEEP PACE WITH
THE TIMES!

HAVEN'T COPPED ON YET, BUT
BY GUM, I NEARLY DID

THE SAME OLD FACES IN BEACH SUITS ARE HERE AGAIN THIS SUMMER

breasts which peer out from their chests at an angle of 90 degrees are merely the Edwardian beauties sporting brassières which have magically become invisible. As for the men who pursue the girls, their bowlers may change to trilbies and then to the bare heads of the post-Second World War period. The flappy bags of the 1920s may gradually contract to the drainpipe pants of the 1960s and then back again to the flappy bags of the 1970s. But it is revealing about the postcard artists that, being men, while they were willing to depict all kinds of female anatomical excesses, they never really exulted in the spectacular physical proportions of the male's erogenous zones.

For the rest, fashions in the broader sense of life-styles changed a great deal on the postcard surface, not so much underneath. Jokes about knobs on the radio changed to jokes about TV mechanics whose tubes suffered a short; cards advising on how to live on 50/– a week altered their figure to a fiver and then to a tenner, but the substance of the joke – that what-ever a man has to live on, if he knows what's what he will spend the bulk of it on fags and booze – remains to this very day. For eighty years or more the characters in the saucy cards have been ogling barmaids, taking Epsom Salts, sizing up chambermaids, getting bitten by crabs and jellyfish in the most exposed situations. When dresses swept the ground, the hunt was on for the girl who revealed an ankle; when hemlines rose the hunt was still on, but now for a glimpse of calf; then the knee, then the thigh. The ambition may have become more grandiloquent, but the attitude has remained identical. The social historian of the future, curious about the conception of one person being 'faster' than another, and anxious to discover in what 'fastness' consisted at various times, could do much worse than consult the delicate seismograph of the postcard artist's sensibilities, his worldly wisdom, his instinctive awareness of how much too far to go in a world which was for ever complaining that things had already gone far enough.

I'M NOT AS YOUNG AS I USED TO BE,
BUT I CAN GIVE THE FLAPPERS
A RUN FOR THEIR MONEY YET

THEY'LL MISS ME NEXT WEEK. HAVE
GIVEN THE GIRLS A WONDERFUL TIME

"THEY'LL NEVER DO IT LASS—**YOU'VE** BEEN TRYING FOR YEARS!"

"AND WHERE ARE YOU THINKING OF **WEARING** THE BRASSIERE MADAM?"

"YOU WOULDN'T **CATCH ME** IN A BIKINI, ALFRED!"
"CATCH YER—**I WOULDN'T EVEN CHASE YOU**, LASS!"

"DON'T YOU EVER GET COLD ON YOUR **BEAT** MISS?"
"NO, SERGEANT— **I WEAR MY BEATNIKS!!**"

"SHE CALLS IT HER **ATOMIC DRESS** IT'S GOT **20%** FALLOUT!"

"PLUNGING NECKLINES, AND SHORTER SKIRTS, I DON'T KNOW WHERE IT'S GOING TO FINISH!"
"**NO—BUT I'D LIKE TO BE AROUND WHEN IT DOES!**"

HOW TO LIVE ON 30/- A WEEK!

	s.	d.
BEER	18	0
WIFE'S BEER	1	6
WEEK'S GRUB	CREDIT	
RENT	SOMETIME	
MID-WEEK BEER	2	6
WIRELESS (HIRE PURCHASE)	2	0
COAL	BORROW IT	
BURIAL CLUB (WIFE)	1	0
PICTURES	1	0
HOLIDAY CLUB	2	0
SIXPENCE EACH WAY	1	0
MORE BEER	2	6
TOTAL ...	£1 - 11	6

THAT MEANS 1/6 IN DEBT, SO
PERSUADE THE WIFE TO BE TEETOTAL!

HOW TO LIVE ON TEN QUID A WEEK!

BEER	£4 - 3 - 0
WIFE'S BEER	2 - 0
CIGARETTES	2 - 10 - 0
WEEK'S GRUB	CREDIT
RENT	OVERDUE
TELEVISION (INSTALMENTS)	19 - 0
MID-WEEK BEER	1 - 5 - 0
COAL	BORROW NEIGHBOURS
CINEMA	9 - 0
FOOTBALL POOLS	10 - 0
BOB EACH WAY	2 - 0
BURIAL CLUB (WIFE)	2 - 0
	£10-2-0

THAT MEANS 2/- IN DEBT, SO
CUT OUT THE WIFE'S BEER!

8
WHO'S LITTLE WILLIE?

By a remarkable coincidence, all the taboo subjects which the Puritan conscience had so morbidly on its mind happened to refer to certain bodily acts without which humanity is incapable of functioning for more than five minutes on end. Quite clearly, it was not in the best interests of things if people went around calling a spade a spade and then laughing about it. It really was a very awkward and distressing business, but there it was. Even a puritan could see that the acts themselves had to be committed if the human race was not to become extinct, for, by some lamentable oversight on the part of the Almighty, even the most devout and passionate puritan owes his existence to one of these vulgar physical acts.

The solution was found not in a total blackout, but in a series of euphemisms which were acceptable in polite society. Sometimes these disguises took the form of some safely abstruse foreign language, as in Gibbon's *The Decline and Fall of the Roman Empire*, in which the more salacious footnotes were expressed in Latin. This tactic holds two curiously contradictory implications: that only very erudite and learned gentlemen have a desire to read of such scandalous goings on, and that it is only the uneducated mob which needs to be protected from itself. However, as both the erudite gentlemen and the uneducated mob were doing all the things in the footnotes anyway, Gibbon's tactfulness made very little difference to the general moral condition of the nation.

A later, typically nineteenth-century refinement was to cloak the naked body in decorous language, so that a harmless old word like 'lavatory' was usurped by 'toilet', even though the latter means something quite different. Women were never pregnant, they were 'with child', or even more asinine, 'in an inter-

THE

FAMILY SHAKSPEARE,

In Eight Volumes;

IN WHICH

NOTHING IS ADDED TO THE ORIGINAL TEXT;

BUT THOSE WORDS AND EXPRESSIONS ARE OMITTED
WHICH CANNOT WITH PROPRIETY BE READ
ALOUD IN A FAMILY.

———— exemit labem purumque reliquit
Æthereum sensum, atque aurai simplicis ignem.
VIRGIL.

BY

THOMAS BOWDLER, Esq. F.R.S. & S.A.

THE FIFTH EDITION.

VOL. I.

CONTAINING
TEMPEST;
TWO GENTLEMEN OF VERONA;
MERRY WIVES OF WINDSOR;
TWELFTH-NIGHT: OR, WHAT YOU WILL;
MEASURE FOR MEASURE;
MUCH ADO ABOUT NOTHING.

esting condition'. A gentleman perspired without ever becoming sweaty, and judges talked of being *in flagrante delicto* – Gibbon again – when what they meant was having a bit on the side. The system worked reasonably well, although sometimes a certain semantic confusion arose, as for instance in the phrase 'breaking wind' which could refer to breaking it either from the stomach or from the back of the beyond. However, the Victorians were willing to accept a little imprecision, so long as standards of decency were maintained.

It should be stressed that no matter how vociferously the Victorians tried to deny it, euphemism had by no means always been the golden rule in educated English society. Indeed, the pre-Victorian Dr Thomas Bowdler, whose pietistic career suggests he believed in the myth of his own immaculate conception, actually made a living out of castrating the texts of those literary works deemed indispensable to a good education and yet too outspoken in their thoughts. Dr Bowdler would not have appreciated being reminded that two of the greatest geniuses in the European literary tradition, Chaucer and Rabelais, had shown the world that farting, being an essentially comic explosion, ought to be laughed at; indeed Rabelais had gone even further and written a most touching domestic ode about a man whose wife kept blowing him out of the bed at night. To all this the Victorians maintained a public face of stony indifference. It was not that they believed the great ones of their world were above such petty bodily acts. I have actually sat on the royal lavatory seat in Queen Victoria's private railway carriage, and can vouch for the admirable practicality of Victorian plumbing arrangements. What was considered *outré* was not the act itself, but the name by which ill-bred people described it.

Perhaps the queen's attitudes best epitomise this curious evasiveness over the essentials of life. With authentic bowdlerian silliness, Victoria was convinced that great art must always keep its buttons done up. In April 1859, having heard that her daughter, the Princess Royal, had been debauching herself by watching Shakespeare, she wrote the girl an anxious letter:

By the by you went to see the Merry Wives*; you must have found it very coarse; even I have never had the courage to go and see it – having always been told how*

very coarse it was – for your adored Shakespeare is dreadful in that respect and many things have to be left out of many of his plays.

And yet Elizabeth Longford in her biography of Victoria refers to 'those who argue that Queen Victoria, with her erotic Hanoverian inheritance, wore out Prince Albert by sheer greediness'. It seems that if only the queen had gone to see a few more performances of *The Merry Wives of Windsor*, and arranged a few less with her husband, Albert might have survived long enough to drive the Prince of Wales completely mad instead of sending him only halfway to distraction. It is all very risible, but then a society which sent its children down the pit-shaft and put trousers on the legs of its grand pianos is perhaps not the best age to look to for a commonsensical morality.

The mass of the English population, no less than their queen, adopted the same double standards in everyday life, defying the call for euphemism in their own verbal exchanges and yet demanding it from the witch-doctors of their society. A physician or a priest or a statesman was expected to display at all times that same pristine vocabulary that the queen had been so bitterly disappointed not to have discovered in Shakespeare. What, one wonders, would have been the fate of a nineteenth-century English politician who dared to behave as his French counterpart did? Edmond de Goncourt, on 17 February 1888, found himself sitting at dinner next to Clemenceau, future premier of France:

He told me some curious anecdotes about the peasants in his province and how they would stop him out in the open during his tours of the department to consult him about their illnesses. He described one huge woman who, just as the horses of his brake were about to gallop away from some place or other, leaned on their cruppers and called out, 'Oh, Monsieur, I suffer from wind something awful!' To which the Radical deputy, giving his horses a crack of the whip which sent them on their way, replied, 'Then fart, my good woman, fart!'

The English were not in a position to borrow those

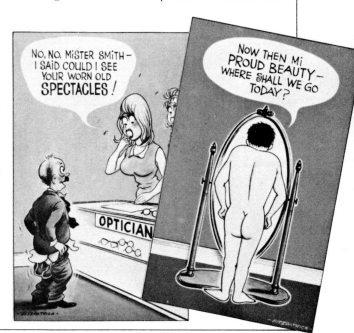

Madam, do you mind making room for my Little Mary?

Have I punched your ticket, Sir?
— — — — Bow-wow!

ENJOYING MYSELF, BUT BOTHERED WI' WIND

tactics. Crazy as it sounds, they could perform the act so eloquently described in de Goncourt's *Journal*, but the moment they described it in print for public consumption they could be prosecuted and sent to prison. So they evolved other tactics.

Accepting the principle of the euphemism they turned it to their own advantage mainly by making the surrogate-word even more comically derisive than the original it was meant to camouflage. A perfect example is the very title of the volume now in the reader's hand. There is no logical reason why the expression 'little Willie' should raise a laugh, but a land plagued with the pestilence of Bowdlers has no alternative but to take its laughter wherever it can find it. The counter-attack was a brilliant affair, most dashingly conducted. It was based on the strategy of the *double entendre*, by which one statement has two meanings, the first salubrious, the second salacious. The beauty of the system is that the moment a Bowdler claims to be scandalised by the salacious remark he can be indicted as a filthy-minded scoundrel for not having interpreted the phrase in its salubrious intent. As late as the 1950s Max Miller was basing his act on this technique. He would, for example, tell audiences the sad tale of the girl who swallowed a pin when she was twelve years old and never felt the prick till she was sixteen, and then wilt in comical horror before the knowing yo-ho's of the congregation.

The music hall was the very cockpit of calculated vulgarity, for it was against its red plush background, with the gilt-painted hamadryads smiling benignly from wedding-cake ceilings, that the ribald determination of the English to call a spade a spade met

head-on with the Polite Conspiracy. Max Miller was not the first artist of the halls to perfect this strategy; on the contrary, posterity will probably see him as the last in a tradition which died at some point in mid-century. No matter who began the campaign, it was certainly Marie Lloyd who elevated it to an art-form, drawing roars of delighted recognition from audiences who knew perfectly well how to decode the lyrics of songs and to blow a concerted raspberry at whichever ninny it was who happened to be filling the post of Lord Chamberlain:

Yes, I've learned to know the bliss
Of a stolen little kiss,
When you heave a sigh and softly murmur, 'Pet!'
As you gaze into his face,
Wrapt in amorous embrace,
But I've never lost my last train yet, Oh, No!
I've never lost my last train yet.

Why the railway should be so prolific a source of suggestiveness and euphemism nobody has bothered to explain, but Marie Lloyd's audiences were certainly the richer for it:

She arrived at Euston by the midnight train,
But when she got to the wicket
There was someone wanted to punch her ticket;
The guards and the porters came round her by the score,
And she told them all that she'd never had her ticket
punched before.

Towards the end of her life, Marie Lloyd, by then one of the most magnificent ruins in the history of English folk-art, actually abandoned euphemism altogether in order to deliver an unequivocal statement to the effect that 'a little bit of what yer fancy does yer

"THAT'S A BATTERED OLD **BRAZIER**, JIM — IT
WON'T LAST MUCH LONGER!"

"HE'S AN ABSOLUTE BOUNDER, HE OUGHT TO BE OSTRACISED!"
"NAY, FANNY—THAT'S GOING A BIT TOO FAR!"

"LADIES AND GENTLEMEN, WHAT WILL YOU OFFER ME FOR
THAT FINE OLD RELIC OVER THERE, WITH **CURVED LEGS**,
AND ROOMY DRAWERS?"

"WHY, MRS. GILES—I THOUGHT I HEARD YOUR HUSBAND
SAY **YOU'D** BROKEN YOUR LEG!!"

A 'BAMFORTH' COMIC

"WHY DON'T YOU DO SOMETHING, GEORGE, CAN'T YOU SEE MY PREDICAMENT?"
"NO, DEAR — **I'VE GOT MY EYES COVERED!**"

"AND FROM HERE, GENTLEMEN, WE GET A MARVELLOUS VIEW OF THE OLD BATTLEMENTS—WHICH, THOUGH REPAIRED, HAVE WITHSTOOD THE SIEGE OF TIME!"

"AYE, SHE'S TOP HEAVY AND SHE WEARS HER FUNNELS TOO HIGH—**BUT SHE'S O.K. FOR PLEASURE!**"

"BLIMEY! I'LL BET **THEM** AIN'T HALF PAINFUL, BERT!"

good', which is after all no less wise than Oscar Wilde's confession that he could resist anything except temptation. But for all her unchallenged eminence as the queen of popular entertainment, Marie was pointedly omitted from the first ever Royal Command Performance because some bowdlerite at Court decided that her vulgarity was too offensive for royal ears. What, then, would some comic postcards of the period have meant to the royal eyes?

Perhaps, after all, the ultra-respectable elements in British society were so innocent that they would have read the line 'I'd like to stick it out here for another week' and thought it was a reference to the pleasures of taking the waters. Perhaps there was a solemn real-life prototype of the wartime mother who boasted about her daughter serving with the troops in France: 'My Fanny's at the front.' Perhaps there really is a dumb blonde somewhere who is convinced that ping-pong balls is the name of an oriental disease, and Moby·Dick its western variant; and perhaps some-were there lives a girl, possibly the same one, who when asked what she thought of Dickens, replied, 'I don't know; I've never been to one.' Somebody had to manufacture those ambivalent lines and it is doubtful that the postcard artists actually invented them; it is more likely that they plucked them out of the air, caught ribaldry on the wing in saloon bars and railway waiting rooms and service clubs, and perhaps in those inexhaustible depositories of dirty laughter, barbers' shops. And then, having polished the best lines, the postcard poets used them for captions, firing the general public's bullets straight back.

Much of the effect of the English *double entendre* has depended on the convenient multiplicity of uses to which the tiny, innocent word 'it' may be put. It is part of the national mythology that when a small man marries a tall lady it is his friends who 'put him up to it', that only the most frustrated swains ever utter the *cri de coeur* 'It's hard when I think of you', that young men who ask young ladies the question, 'If I let something slip out, will you hold it against me?' are not always thinking about the acceptability of their smalltalk. For the rest, the *double entendre* postcard leans heavily on the little-Willie syndrome. Probably they will prove to be immortal, the jokes about my friend Dick, about the people holding an Oddfellows' Ball, about keeping abreast of the times, about strok-ing pussies to keep them warm, about writing love letters and putting lots of kisses on the bottom, about the small boy who overheard his father say to his mother at bedtime 'Let's put out the candle and have a bit' and naturally assumed he must be an Eskimo. It is that split second of comprehension which sparks off the laughter, and it may well be that postcards not-withstanding, the appreciation of the kind of sallies I mention is at its best a communal affair.

One night I attended the Victoria Palace to watch the Crazy Gang. Even as I sat there admiring their technique and revelling in their astonishing profess-ional longevity, something told me that an epoch was passing, that I would never see them in action again and that their like would never pass this way in the future. I wondered that night if anything any of them said would stick in my memory without my realising it at the time. Something did, and it was like seeing a comic postcard suddenly burst into life. The house erupted in great crashing waves of laughter, and the Polite Conspiracy had been foiled once again. 'He's a eunuch,' explained Bud Flanagan with diocesan solemnity, 'he's got no scruples.'

The Crazy Gang – without scruples

"MAKE IT HALF-A-DOZEN, LADY!"

"THEY'VE SCRATCHED MRS. DOLITTLE'S PEGASUS!"
"WELL TELL HER TO PUT SOME IODINE ON IT!"

"CAN YOU DO ANYTHING ABOUT MY SEAT MISTER? IT KEEPS WOBBLING UP AND DOWN!"

"THERE'S QUITE A LOT HERE MR. TWIDDLE!"
"THERE CERTAINLY IS!!"

BLIMEY!!

"AUNTIE'S UP AT THE TOP, AND MUM'S DOWN AT THE BOTTOM!"
"YOU'RE DEAD RIGHT, LADDIE!"

"IS THE WIND TROUBLING YOU MISSUS?"
"YES, BUT I'LL BE ALRIGHT WHEN THE BAND STARTS TO PLAY!"

"IF YOU WERE A LADY—YOU'D KNOCK ON THE DOOR!"
"—AND IF YOU WERE A GENTLEMAN YOU'D STAND UP WHEN A LADY ENTERS THE ROOM!"

"YOU CAN'T BEAT A BIRD WITH A NICE MEATY CHEST, BERT!"

117

9
DOMESTIC BLISS

Those scruples, or rather, what Bud Flanagan had in mind when he referred to them, were part of the essential equipment for a man in his entry into the hopelessly one-sided war of the sexes. However, in entering the world of the traditional British working-class marriage, we should be careful to temper our laughter with scepticism, because although the termagant with the rampant rolling pin and the frostbitten nose undoubtedly did exist, she never existed quite as exclusively as she does in the never-never land of the comic postcard. In fact, in studying the graphic fables of this section, we are entering one of the most notorious of all male chauvinist piggeries, an area where the depiction of life is coloured by the fact that not only were all the artists, caption writers, editors and retailers men, but so were most of the customers. What makes the postcard representation of domestic bliss unique in the context of this anthology is the fact that it is the one section that girls, ladies and old women will not be particularly inclined to laugh at.

Consider the world placed before us. Very often the size, the physical bulk of the two parties to the marital contract has undergone a bizarre metamorphosis which symbolises the sad imbalance between romance and reality, between the expectation of Rabelaisian nights and the ultimate condition of drudging days. Presumably the weight advantage should have gone all the other way, because if, as we are constantly told by the postcard artists, the male swigged beer while his helpmeet stayed home and bit on the furniture, either in rage or conjugal frustration, then it should have been the male whose gut became distended and his partner who withered away. Masculine propaganda has reversed this. It is a contradiction which has never been questioned, and

which is bedevilled by the fact that very often the working-class wife really did swell into the elephantine nightmare of the postcard artists.

But there is a deeper and much sadder mystery. What happened to all the randy swains who pursued busty grinning girls down the labyrinth of bachelor days? And what happened to all the busty grinning girls they pursued? Look at the face of the archetypal wife, that militant ascetic ready to clobber with the blunt instrument of her disenchantment the slightest tendency of the male to enjoy himself. Look at her, the embodiment of misanthropic intent, a tartar in whose bloodstream the milk of human kindness long ago became polluted by the vinegar of self-denial. What happened to her sexual appetite and her plebeian genius for saucy stratagems? How and why should it be that her husband, who chased her until she caught him, has declined from a ruttish paramour to a kind of humanoid hot-water bottle with cold feet, sexually as well as physically speaking? Of all the depressing things about the postcard delineation of working-class life, the most depressing is that very often the elements of tragedy lurk behind the laughter. The existence the cards depict may appear hilarious in retrospect to the onlooker, but it must have been wretched to the brink of hell for the principals at the time.

The truth is that there was an unarguable case for the marauding puritanism of those wives, a case which is never explicitly argued in the comic literature of the period, and which indeed was barely hinted at even in the most serious fiction before the twentieth century. Baldly, the working-class female came to fear and eventually to abhor sex because it meant more children. In the teeming warrens of my childhood, I can recollect not one but several families within a half-mile radius which could, and once or twice a year actually did, field their own football teams, usually with a couple of reserves. The matriarch, prematurely old, her energy sapped, her juices dry, her facial integument drained to the hue and texture of damp cardboard, would recruit the eldest to tend to the youngest while she rested gnarled elbows on first-floor window-sills on summer nights, waiting for the flower of the district's manhood to pour itself out of the saloon bars at eleven o'clock. She was, of course, no more confused and disappointed by it all than her partner who, defeated by his own bewilderment at the unexpected turn that events appeared to have taken, would stand with his foot on the rail of the Lord Nelson or the Valiant Trooper, exchanging scraps of moth-eaten philosophy and staring through eyes rendered thyroid by the beer at the wrinkled, shrinking princes of his long-vanished youth.

The postcard artists, when they drew comic inspiration from such scenes, usually left out two of the most striking groups of characters in the tableau: the wives themselves, who very often, and particularly on Saturday night, went drinking with the old man, and the prancing troupes of small children, left to their own resources just outside the pub door. There they sported with cream soda and over-salted crisps, barred by the licensing laws from going inside and getting as drunk as the old man; and inevitably coming to associate maturity with the right to buy a drink. To have made too much of a point of all this would have been to smudge the battle-lines of the war of the sexes. It had, for the sake of an easy laugh, to be hedonists versus killjoys, life-livers against life-deniers, piss-artists ranged against sobersides. And so

MIND YOU DON'T MUCKY YOUR TICKET!

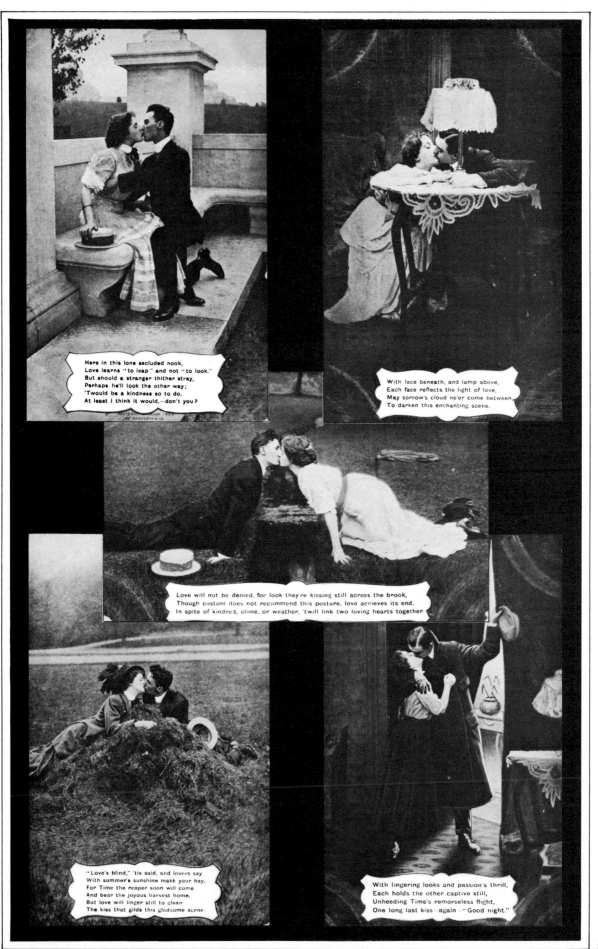

Here in this lone secluded nook,
Love learns "to leap" and not "to look."
But should a stranger thither stray,
Perhaps he'll look the other way;
'Twould be a kindness so to do,
At least I think it would,—don't you?

With lace beneath, and lamp above,
Each face reflects the light of love,
May sorrow's cloud ne'er come between,
To darken this enchanting scene.

Love will not be denied, for look they're kissing still across the brook,
Though custom does not recommend this posture, love achieves its end,
In spite of kindred, clime, or weather, 'twill link two loving hearts together.

"Love's blind," 'tis said, and lovers say
With summer's sunshine make your hay,
For Time the reaper soon will come
And bear the joyous harvest home,
But love will linger still to glean
The kiss that gilds this gladsome scene.

With lingering looks and passion's thrill,
Each holds the other captive still,
Unheeding Time's remorseless flight,
One long last kiss—again—"Good night."

the all-male preserve of the comic postcard, that most spectacular of propaganda weapons, resolutely rigged the facts. The student hoping to compile a representative anthology of comic postcards showing the husband clobbering the wife with a rolling pin has a long search before him.

The male advocate would probably have replied that it is this very reversal of roles in the sex war, with the woman become the attacker, which makes the whole thing funny. We can laugh at the timorous male doing the washing-up, but what of the timorous female? All this is true, but it does not alter the fact that when violence was done in working-class homes, with or without rolling pins, it was usually the wife who ended up on the wrong end of the assault. Of course, every working-class child can look back on the spectacle of a few local battle-axes who terrorised the male into docility. I can see one or two of them in my mind's eye even now, formidable manifestations of controlled belligerence sailing through the crooked back streets of St Marylebone like galleons in a duck-pond, proud in the knowledge that whatever the legal position, no mere husband was ever going to tell them where to get off – or even, as Max Miller might have added, how to get on. Small boys instinctively gave

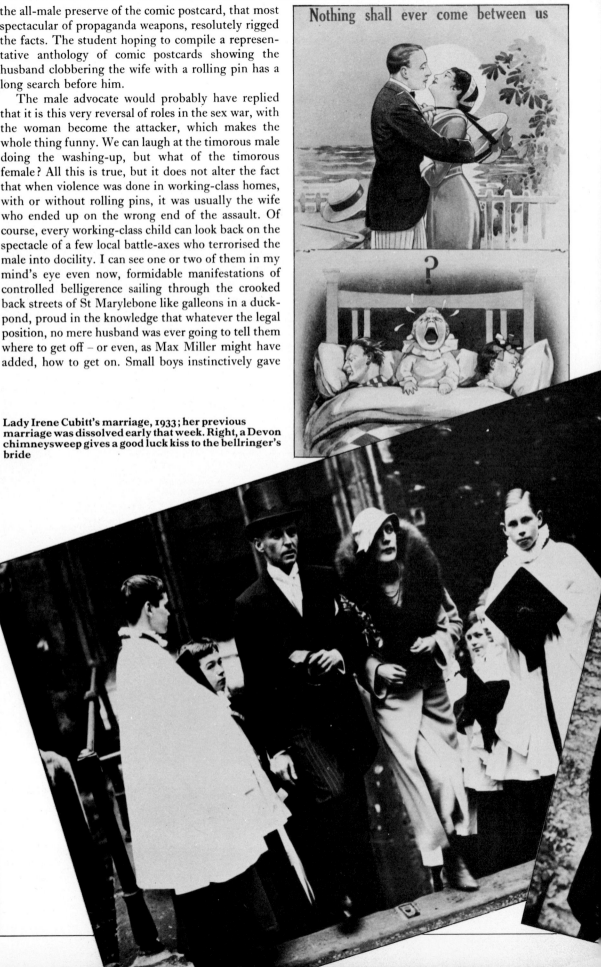

Nothing shall ever come between us

Lady Irene Cubitt's marriage, 1933; her previous marriage was dissolved early that week. Right, a Devon chimneysweep gives a good luck kiss to the bellringer's bride

a wide berth to these slum valkyries, and would get out of the way whenever one was spied drifting along the pavement. We might have flung apple-cores and tin cans at them, but only from the sanctity of a doorway or a range of fifteen yards, after which we would all resolve not to get married before our two hundred and fiftieth birthdays at the very least. We would ponder the phenomenon of beards on female chins and warts on female noses and carbuncles on female feet and alarming signs of approaching baldness on female scalps and tell ourselves that perhaps after all there were more pitfalls in this life than they told you about.

But we knew that these were the exceptions, and that this was still unmistakably a man's world. When it came to a clash of wills, it was the husband who always held the ultimate deterrent. He usually had what money there was, and there was nothing, in either the written or the unwritten laws of life, to force him to hand any of it over, or even disclose how much of it there was. A vast number of the hard-done-by men in these comic postcards were actually defrauding their own wives and children by never revealing how much, if anything, they earned. One of the saddest sketches in the working-class theatre of reality used to be the Argument Without End, where she would ask him for money to buy the food and he would say he didn't have any and she would say he *must* have some and he would say he didn't and neither party ever found out if the other was telling the truth. No inkling of this kind of oppression comes over in the postcards, which seem to anticipate by several hundred years the day when the triumph of Women's Liberation is complete.

And yet, in spite of the appalling plight of husbands who very often could not find work even when they went looking for it, and of wives who very often could not find husbands no matter now hard they went looking for them, the institution of the working-class family withstood the storms of circumstances with what appears to have been amazing fortitude. All those breezy chaps who had dashed to the altar in the pathetic belief that the marriage ceremony was sanction for an orgy without end, and then found themselves handling babies who seemed to consist in their entirety of leaky orifices, all those giggly girls who hadn't been able to choose the ring quickly enough because they saw it as their release from work, only to find themselves doing a ninety-hour week with no wages at all – why did they not simply cut and run,

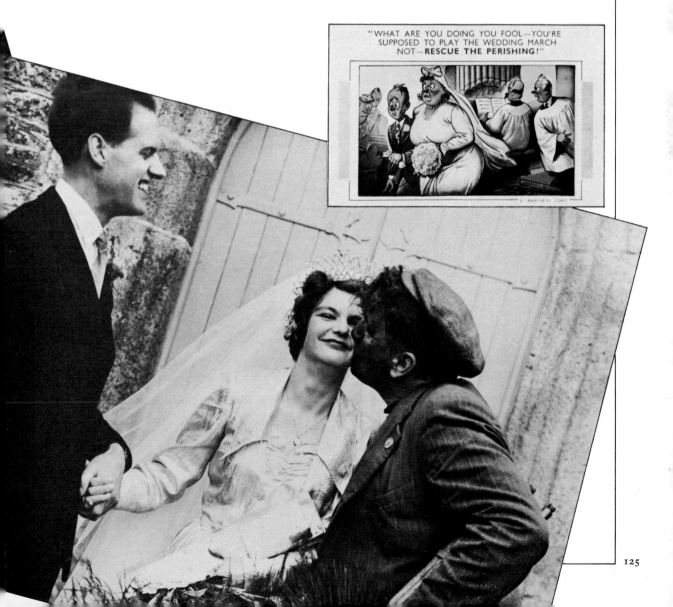

"WHAT ARE YOU DOING YOU FOOL—YOU'RE SUPPOSED TO PLAY THE WEDDING MARCH NOT—**RESCUE THE PERISHING!**"

in their millions? For a partner who snores is one thing, but when the plaster comes flaking down from the bedroom ceiling it is quite another. To marry a dainty maid seems good sense, but surely it constitutes fraudulent conversion when she then transforms herself into a twenty-stone avenging angel whose amorphous mass defies all the ingenuities of priapic expertise? The problem is preserved for ever now in the amber of Miller's joke about the husband who dreams romantic dreams one night and makes advances to his enormous wife, who wakes indignant, shouting, 'Here, here,' prompting the pathetic response from her eager but totally disorientated partner, 'Where, where?'

Middle-class writers have lavished vast amounts of sentimentality on the humdrum poetry of such marriages, praising the stoic durability of the knocked-about wives and the henpecked husbands. For all their excesses and their philistinism, the theorists inform us, the working classes got on with their lives, raised large familes on a shoe-string, and often on no string at all, and contrived somehow to survive. Whatever eles you said about them, went the lecture, they did at least stick together, observing the marriage vows with far more literal faith than their upper-class counterparts, who divorced and re-married with a flippancy reflected so elegantly in the novels of Evelyn Waugh and Anthony Powell.

The Great Unwashed, however, had never heard of artists like Waugh and Powell, and indeed knew almost nothing of the sentimental regard for working-class qualities which can be found in the essays of that otherwise astute Old Etonian George Orwell. In fact, it was my experience that the working classes to a great extent actually despised the very qualities of dogged commitment for which the sentimental intellectuals praised and envied them. The husbands and wives in the wars of the comic postcards sensed that what the outsider might think was a stoic sense of honour was really no more than a bovine inability to stir the emotional stumps. In any case, the divorces available to the likes of Babs Stringham and Mrs Beste-Chetwynde were withheld from the majority of the population because of one simple factor, shortage of ready money. The would-be working-class Bluebeard was disinherited, as it were, by a lack of wherewithal to collect partners. It is perfectly true that until the great social upheavals of the years after

"DOES THE STORK STILL BRING OUR BABIES, DADDY ?"
"HE USED TO DO, SON—NOW HE SHOUTS DOWN THE
CHIMNEY, **HEY YOU—COME AND GET IT!**"

"SORRY I BOUGHT THAT **ELECTRIC WASHER**, FRED;
THE WIFE GOT CAUGHT IN THE ROLLERS AND
NOW SHE **CAN'T FEED THE BABY!**"

"YOU'RE A BORN KIDDER, FRED,—YOU ALLUS HAVE BEEN!"

"I THOUGHT YOU SAID IT WAS A TALKING PARROT!"
"IT IS—BUT IT'S LIKE ME—**IT CAN'T GET A BLINKING WORD IN EDGEWAYS!**"

"IS YOUR OLD MAN GOING TO HAVE ONE?"

the Second World War most working-class marriage partners stuck together, but the adhesive which worked the trick so effectively was not constancy but penury. Had you approached any of the disgruntled characters in these comic postcards and asked them if they had ever considered divorce, they would have paused in the execution of their ceaseless guerrilla war, gazed at you with hostile contempt and probably told you to mind your own business. You might just as well have asked them what they were wearing for Royal Ascot next season or if they were happy with the performance of their investment broker. The poor never went in for divorce because they were the poor, and couldn't afford such fripperies. Just as mutual detestation often turned out to be their most effective method of contraception, so their mutual neediness became their guarantee of a curious kind of guarded emotional security.

Naturally they evolved certain alternatives to divorce, alternatives commensurate with the maintenance of dignity, or keeping up appearances as it was laughingly described. They went in quite a bit for the *ménage à trois*, which sometimes had the added advantage of spreading the burden of the rent; there were several fancy women, as well as a sizable shifting population of aunts whose blood-ties with the nieces and nephews whose heads they uneasily patted were nebulous to say the very least. There were, in other words, accommodations, but almost never was there the juridical formality of a divorce. The henpecked husband and the shrewish wife were chained together for ever by the prohibitive cost of a locksmith. It was as simple as that. Probably the two greatest factors in the geometrical progression of divorce statistics in the last thirty years have nothing much to do with the loosening of morals or corsets, and a great deal to do with Hollywood and the Marriage Guidance Councils which informed the masses of the existence of divorce, and Legal Aid, which showed them how to pay for it. As for the indignities heaped on the heads of the well-intentioned husbands in these postcards, not only are they no longer true now, but they were only half-true then, for which reason they are funny, sometimes oddly moving, and also largely moonshine. The one absolutely accurate feature about them is the eternal presence of small, scruffy children, unwitting jailors of mothers and fathers who, had they been able to afford it, might otherwise have flown the coop long before.

ONE HOME.

TWO AWAY.

THREE RIGHT ON HIS COUPON!

"WHAT'S UP, MAC---ANYTHING WRONG?"
"AYE! THE WIFE'S HAD AN OPERATION---SHE SWALLOWED HALF-A-CROON, AND THERE'S NO CHANGE YET!"

"MY LITTLE GRETA GARBO!"
"OH, MY OWN RONALD COLMAN!"

LOVE IS BLIND
(PERHAPS IT'S AS WELL)

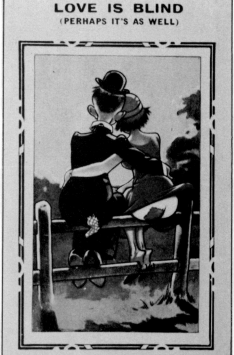

A FELLOW WHO HELPS HIMSELF TO MEAT LIKE THIS OUGHT TO BE A MEMBER OF HALF-A-DOZEN MUSTARD CLUBS!

I'd a fine exshcuse for the misshus
to-night—but that bomb's knocked it
out of my head.

Is that you, John? What're you doing?
I was just wondering how that jazz step
goes, dearie!

I come here often—the change does me good!

GO ON, MRS. HIGGINS, .I'M ALL EARS!

"THOSE ARE HIS ASHES DEARIE, HE NEVER DID A STROKE OF WORK WHEN HE WAS ALIVE—BUT NOW HE'S TIMING EGGS WHETHER HE LIKES IT OR NOT!"

"E' LOVE—THE GRATE'S A BIT OLD FASHIONED—BUT THE FIRE'S STILL BURNING!"

BLIMEY!

10
THE LITTLE DARLINGS

At this point, with the working-class husband and wife locked in the passionate embrace of two all-in wrestlers intent on dislocating each other's jaws, we arrive at the solution of the mystery which persists in at least half the comic post-cards ever printed, the eternal presence of fat ladies. Their vulgarity, and the matching coarseness of their mates, was something which greatly exercised Orwell in his discovery of the world of McGill, and led him to compose an inventory of what he found:

Sex-appeal vanishes at about the age of twenty-five. Well-preserved and good-looking people beyond their first youth are never represented. The amorous honey-mooning couple reappear as the grim-visaged wife and shapeless, moustachioed, red-nosed husband, no inter-mediate stage being allowed for.

Later in the same essay he returns to his puzzling theme, noting that

There are no pictures, or hardly any, of good-looking people beyond their first youth.
There is the 'spooning' couple and the middle-aged, cat-and-dog couple, but nothing in between. The liaison, the illicit but more or less decorous love-affair which used to be the stock joke of French comic papers, is not a post-card subject. And this reflects, on a comic level, the work-ing-class outlook which takes it as a matter of course that youth and adventure – almost, indeed, individual life – end with marriage. One of the few authentic class-differ-ences, as opposed to class-distinctions, still existing in England is that the working classes age very much earlier. They do not live less long, provided they survive their childhood, nor do they lose their physical activity earlier, but they do lose very much earlier their youthful appear-ance.

And the reason why they lost it was simply their con-

MENACE
of the
EMPTY
Cradle

The "one child only" habit is growing, but many married people prefer the pleasures of life to parenthood

By A. G. GARDINER

IT is said that "the hand that rocks the cradle rules the world." But that maxim assumes that there is a baby in the cradle. To-day it is the empty cradle that haunts the mind of nearly every civilised society.

We have been late in taking alarm at the menace of depopulation that overhangs the white races. France has for years been struggling to stop the famine of babies. Mussolini in Italy has been as active in inducing Italian women to breed more children as he has been in massacring the women and children of Abyssinia.

Hitler in Germany has been equally clamorous for more babies. In Sweden the Government has set the statisticians to discover the causes and remedies of a depopulation that fills them with panic.

As long ago as 1903 the Government of New South Wales appointed a Commission to enquire into a declining birth-rate that was "sapping the vitals

based are indisputable. If they continue to operate the conclusion will "follow as the night the day." Fifty years ago the birth-rate in this country was 34 per thousand of the population. Forty years ago it was 30 per thousand; twenty years ago 25 per thousand. Last year it was 14.8 per 1,000.

Thus in one generation the output of babies per 1,000 of the population has been more than halved.

The significance of this tremendous social fact has been obscured by an almost equivalent fall in the death rate. In 1880 the rate was 20 per 1,000; last year it was 12 per 1,000. Roughly, the decline in the death-rate has balanced the decline in the birth-rate.

But that balance cannot be tained. Births, as Dr. McC

and I do not personally prop... awake at night...

ments in t... almost cer... With all... the empty... race suicide... State are fee...

"WOULD YOU LIKE A LITTLE BASKET MISSUS?"

"NO THANKS MISTER, I'VE GOT ONE!"

HAND MADE BASKET

stant harassment by the great teeming armies of their own descendants. Pregnancy and childbirth were the two vital experiences which inflated those slender virginal hussies into the great mountains of marauding blubber whose brooding presence dominates the postcard world. Of course post-natal obesity is by no means an inevitable consequence of one night of love, but it was for the working-class mothers of fifty, sixty, eighty years ago, earth-mothers who knew no more effective therapy for the restoration of the wasp-waist than to keep the elbow bent till the glass was empty. And the fatter the lady, the more children we were expected to deduce. In fact, we could deduce further, and suggest that of the two most common mature female types in the world of the vulgar post-card, it was the fat lady who was understood to have a firm grasp of the principles of copulation, and the 'grim-visaged wife' of Orwell's troubled view who had somehow missed out on that particular sort of diversion.

The offspring of those fat ladies, the mischievous and unprincipled sprites drawn by McGill, Taylor, Tempest and company, were born into middle-sized clubs, juvenile mafiosa consisting entirely of their own brothers and sisters. They wore one another's boots, pilfered one another's privileges, slept in one another's beds, and came to the discovery of the myriad orifices in the universe with the pride of the intrepid explorer who has stumbled on a wonderful secret. Study their cheerfully amoral faces; they are a persistently grubby lot, more or less uneducable, untrustworthy, ravening little beasts interested only in the gratification of their own appetites. They are armoured against the hypocritical pietism of their

BETWEEN YOU AND ME AND THE GATEPOST   A SATURDAY FEATURE

The HAPPY QUIVER-FULL

LARGE AND HEALTHY FAMILIES DESERVE PRAISE —AND SOMETHING MORE

SAYS THE TALLYMAN :

A REAL HAPPY FAMILY. — Here are ten of a family of fourteen children with their mother, Mrs. Orton, of 3, Richmond-avenue, Leicester. From back to front: Jack (aged 20 years), Pat (18), Nancy (16), Mairwen (14), Doreen (13), Peggy (12), Trevor (8), Marjorie (6), David (5), Leslie (2) and Mrs. Orton.

"I EXPECTED YOUR NEW BABY TO HAVE LONG EARS Mrs. SMITH—MY DAD SAYS YOU BREED 'EM LIKE RABBITS!"

elders by an instinctive grasp of that priceless item of child-awareness, the fact that our parents are really no better than we are, but only marginally more cunning in concealing the fact. Not a very promising prospect for the future of the race, but at least a view of childhood more acceptable than the old Victorian flapdoodle about all children being little angels, and less offensive by far than the idiocy which insists that all children are born into a condition of original sin. The passion which informs the kids in the postcards is not original sin at all, but its diametric opposite, original innocence. It is the kind of innocence that can see no reason why the fundamental comicality of a fart should not be acknowledged openly, and that not only regards nose-picking as a harmless if highly refined art, but can spoil the fun of adults who are attempting surreptitiously to practise it by advising them in a loud voice, in mixed company, 'You wanna be careful how you aim that stuff about'.

Why did the fat ladies and their long-suffering husbands keep on producing all the little Willies, to say nuffink of the Johnnies and Alfies and Violets and

MOTHER SAYS TOO MANY TARTS DONT AGREE WITH LITTLE BOYS.

YOU'RE A VERY LOVABLE BOY BUT—YOU'RE VERY VERY SLOW.

SCOUT NOTE—
WHILE ON OUTPOST DUTY KEEP YOUR EYES OPEN & MISS NOTHING.

THE RETURN OF THE SWALLOW.

Jeans and Harrys and Henriettas? Why did they not arrange their affairs more judiciously? Briefly, because they either could not be bothered, or did not know how. H. G. Wells opened the imaginary biography of one of his working-class heroes with the insistence that

It is doubtful if his reluctant entry into this fierce universe would have occurred had it not been for the extreme inadequacy of the knowledge of what are called preventatives in the late Victorian period. People didn't want children then, except by heart's desire, but they got them nevertheless. One knew there was some sort of knowledge about it, but one couldn't be too careful whom one asked, and your doctor also in those days couldn't be too careful in misunderstanding your discreet hints and soundings. In those days England was far behind Polynesia in that matter. So there you were – and do what you could, you were liable to be caught.

The population of Great Britain increased by 300 per cent in the course of the nineteenth century, and yet a million tracts on birth control were sold in the same period; the awareness of the possibilities of contraception slowly filtered down through the national consciousness, from the aristocracy through to the middle classes and eventually to the workers. In 1906 Sidney Webb, Fabian theorist, announced that between half and two-thirds of married couples were practising some form of birth control, and by 1913 *The Times* was running anxious articles about the declining birthrate. Could it be, wondered Printing House Square, that there was 'a general decline in fertility amongst Western civilised nations?' The idea was fatuous; what was really worrying *The Times* was a decline in fertility that was not general but particular, a decline which seemed to many people to point to the eventual triumph of the herd over the élite. For the realisation that children need not be a con-

comitant of lovemaking had hit the better-placed first, so that the pages of *Burke's Peerage* revealed the following statistics with regard to childbearing among the aristocracy:

1840:	*7·1 births per fertile couple*				
1860:	*6·1*	*,,*	*,,*	*,,*	*,,*
1880:	*4·3*	*,,*	*,,*	*,,*	*,,*
1890:	*3·1*	*,,*	*,,*	*,,*	*,,*

If we digest those figures in the light of the Establishment's rampant opposition in those years to the propagandists on behalf of birth control, we glimpse a comical picture of the makers of morals practising those rites among themselves which they deemed disgusting among the Great Unwashed. The fools at *The Lancet* declared that birth control was 'a distasteful subject', while even bigger fools like a certain Major Darwin of the Eugenics lobby demanded the sterilisation of the poor by 'harmless and painless X-rays'. History does not record what eventually happened to Major Darwin, but the real concern of thinkers like him is best expressed in the brief but revealing exchange reported by E. M. Forster in *Howards End*. It shows how people were torn between the belief that England's greatness was somehow linked with her rise in population, and the fear that the wrong sort of people were being born:

'*Evening, Mr. Bast.*'

'*Evening, Mr. Cunningham.*'

'*Very serious thing this decline in the birthrate in Manchester.*'

'*I beg your pardon?*'

'*Very serious thing this decline of the birthrate in Manchester,*' repeated Mr. Cunningham, tapping the Sunday paper, in which the calamity in question had just been announced to him.

May farver be taken for munitions, and muvver for window cleaning, or somefing!

Another Air Raid!

WATCH ADOLF TREMBLE, SISTER!

SOMETHING ACCOMPLISHED, SOMETHING DONE, HAS EARNED A NIGHT'S REPOSE!

TWOSOMES IS LOVELY!

LIFE IS JUST ONE DARNED THING AFTER ANOTHER!

IT'S O.K. WITH ME, KID!

When a man's married his troubles begin.

"AND WHAT WOULD YOU LIKE FOR YOUR BIRTHDAY JOHNNY!"

"I'D LIKE A NICE BLONDE, DAD. BUT I SUPPOSE I'LL GET A RUDDY SPACE GUN!"

"COME ON ALBERT—TELL THE GENTLEMAN WHERE **YOU'VE PUT** YOUR SIXPENCE!"

A 'BAMFORTH' COMIC

'Ah, yes,' said Leonard, who was not going to let on that he had not bought a Sunday paper.

'If this kind of thing goes on the population of England will be stationary in 1960.'

'You don't say so.'

'I call it a very serious thing, eh?'

'Good evening, Mr. Cunningham.'

'Good evening, Mr. Bast.'

Meanwhile, the working classes, unaware that more genteel folk considered a declining birth rate a sure sign of impending national calamity, were doing what they could to induce it to decline even more steeply. A more direct comment than Forster's oblique duologue is the one which came booming out across the footlights of a hundred music halls, a message delivered by a formidable spokeswoman called Lily Morris, who advised, in one of the wisest popular songs ever written:

Don't have any more, Mrs. Moore,
Mrs. Moore, please don't have any more.
The more you have the more you want, they say,
And enough is as good as a feast any day.
If you have any more, Mrs. Moore,
You'll have to take the house next door.
They're all right when they're here
But take my advice my dear,
Don't have any more, Mrs. Moore.

It hardly needs to be said that Lily Morris was one of Nature's fat ladies, or that her advice was being taken all over Britain. For the masses were resolved that what was good enough for Burke's Peerage was certainly good enough for them; when Wells placed the turn-of-the-century English behind Polynesia eugenically speaking, he was perhaps not quite right after all. Before the end of the century birth control was already beginning to have its curbing effect on the proliferating little Willies of England. Sir Neville Cardus, who was born in 1889, remembers studying as a small boy a puzzling conversational exchange between two of his aunts, admirable young women who were fully paid-up members of what Cardus with characteristically Victorian gallantry prefers to call 'the oldest profession':

Every evening after work at the ironing board of an indoor laundry, my wonderful Aunt Beatrice would doll herself up glamorously, belladonna in the eyes, rouge on her cheeks, feather boa, silk stockings, petticoats just to be glimpsed. And she would proceed to, or sail down, Manchester's Oxford Street, to 'pick up'. One evening she returned to our tenement, crying out, 'My God, Jessie, I've forgotten me French letter.' I was puzzled by this statement, because, child though I was, I knew that my Aunt Beatrice did not understand French.

It is worth noting that in Lily Morris's hymn there occurs the statement that 'they're all right when they're here', which seems to imply that if by some error of planning or through sheer oversight or carelessness or excess of drunken passion a little Willie did arrive in the world, he was sure to be greeted with parental tenderness. This was putting rather too soft a face on it. Many of the Willies in the postcards are juveniles who have just had, or are just about to have, their bottoms warmed by some irate parent. And as almost all these young children ever seem to be contemplating are the mechanics of excreting or the pleasures of digestion, that is not surprising. What is downright astonishing is that couples who considered the martyrdom of raising a family too messy an affair preferred to wipe up after a dog instead. It is often said that the presence of a cosseted pooch in the modern family is a sure sign of sterility or impotence or both somewhere in the family, but in my own childhood, dogs usually seemed to be an adjunct to the small children rather than a substitute for them.

It was inevitable that dogs should have attracted the postcard artists, for a dog can perform with ease all the disgusting acts of which a small child is capable, with the added advantage of performing them much more frequently. The possibilities of lamp-posts and tree stumps have proved endless, and it is a staple fact in the armoury of most comedians that even on acquiring maturity, dogs still tend to make love in the most exposed social situations. But the aspect of dog-life which I have always found most attractive in my years as a flabbergasted son of the proletariat is the tendency which the working classes have to imbue their four-legged friends with the same intellectual and artistic qualities which, if they encountered them in their own cousin or mother-in-law, they would spurn with glorious profanity. Most of

the mean streets of my childhood housed at least one old widower convinced that his Airedale could play 'Annie Laurie' on the harmonium, or a shrivelled little spinster who had passed all the nights since the death of Edward VII teaching her cat to dance a quadrille. The claims were not altogether bogus, for the parrot which lived in the flat next to mine when I was a schoolboy eventually reached the stage where it would hear me come down the basement steps and echo the favourite speech of my mother, 'Stop it, Ben'. It is this animal precociousness, rather than jokes about doing the pools or the supply of free manure, which has always attracted me most in the work of the postcard artists. What volumes of love unspoken, what implications of countless days and nights of tuition, are represented by the drawing of the man outflanked by his own success. There sits this devoted animal trainer playing draughts with a brown-and-white mongrel whose head is resting on his own paw rather in the manner of one of Thurber's canine misanthropes. 'My gosh,' says the astonished

onlooker, 'that's a clever dog you've got there.' To which its owner, exasperated beyond measure by the implied insult to his own intellectual powers, and perhaps wishing he had never seen a draughts-board, replies indignantly, 'Oh, I wouldn't say that, mister, I've beaten him twice.'

It is the kind of social predicament which could be resolved in only one way, where man and dog repair together to the nearest saloon bar to share the pleasures of the bottle. In the working-class environment of my childhood, foam on a dog's jaws was less likely to indicate lunacy than a taste for milk stout.

GEE! WOULDN'T I LIKE TO SIT ON SOME NICE GIRL'S LAP.

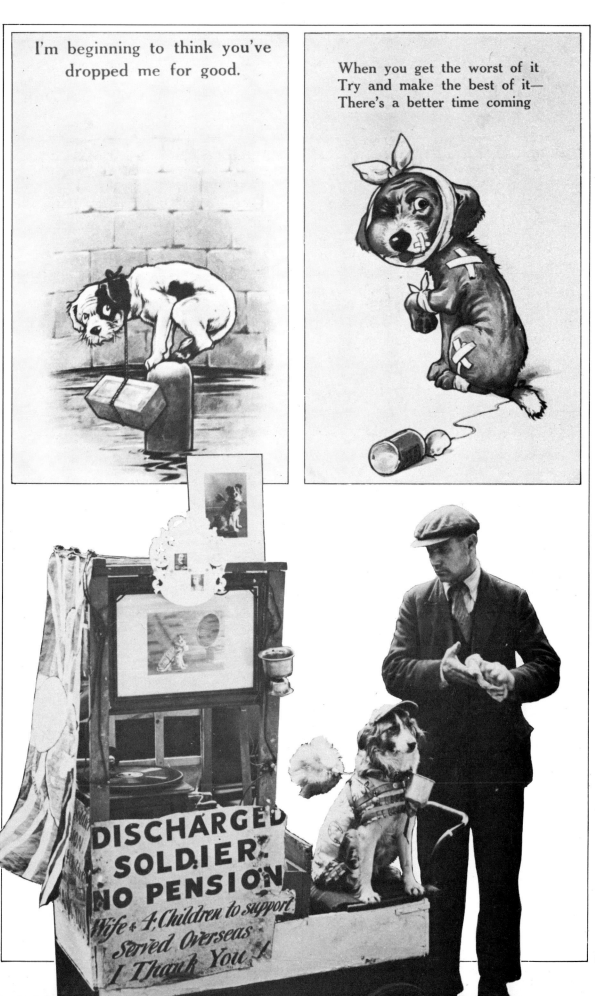

11
LEANING ON A
LAMP-POST

People will always drink. That is the very simplest of propositions, verifiable in ten thousand different ways. It may not be a very desirable proposition, but that does not make it any less true, and its truth is so obvious that even a professional legislator ought to be able to see it. In fact, the social history of Britain in the last 150 years is liberally strewn with the bleached bones of those who either refused to admit the validity of the theory to themselves or, having done so, refused to admit it to anyone else. There were those who saw the admission of the inevitability of some consumption of alcohol as a Christian blasphemy, others who regarded it as an unpatriotic indulgence, others who described it as a moral outrage, still others who saw it as an impediment to industrial prosperity. But whether the Drys were concerned with saving souls or saving the nation or securing a sober work force, their strategy remained

the same. They strove for legislative measures to make the consumption of any alcohol by anybody in any place a physical impossibility.

Of course the chances of achieving this were remote, so their practical policy devolved into a game whose object was to make drinking a little more difficult, a little more inconvenient, a little less comfortable. If they could induce the harassment of a publican here, the closure of a public house there, if they could stiffen the resolve of the occasional Watch Committee or convert the occasional member of Parliament, then a small victory would have been achieved. And it must be admitted that there were moments in English history when they did succeed in snatching victory from the jaws of defeat by snatching alcoholic beverages from the jaws of would-be imbibers; having done so, they stood up proudly to receive the applause of the Liberal conscience. Only a boor would deny them their honour, but it may be as well to remember that the only reason their assault took the decorous legislative form it did was because the laws of the land frowned upon more militant methods; had things been otherwise, the Abolitionists would gladly have slipped black mambas in the beer barrels, sawn the legs off taproom tables, sold brewers' drayhorses for cats' meat, and done all they could to bring life to the point reached by P. G. Wodehouse's Hash Todhunter when he came to resemble 'one who has drained the sour ale of life and found a dead mouse at the bottom of the pewter'.

But no sooner was the Abolitionist banner raised than a rival army, of an even more ferocious moral aspect, sprang up to defend unto death the in-alienable right of every true-born Englishman to drink himself into a soggy grave if that happened to be his desire. These defenders of the alcoholic faith were ready to concede that perhaps the spectacle of the richest empire in history with its streets littered by *bon viveurs* unable to maintain a per-pendicular position did have its regret-table aspects. But, they countered, surely what was far more important was the preservation of the liberty of the individual from the encroachments of a bunch of pussyfooting old ladies? The passion with which the Wets flung themselves into this breach is one of the most gallant features of British history between Waterloo and El-Alamein. They positively trembled with outraged virtue for the sanctity of the Saloon Bar, fought like tigers to guard the rights of the common drunken man, and never once flinched from the assaults of those divines who took too liter-ally Byron's juxtaposition of sermons and soda water. They battled valiantly and honourably to preserve what they believed to be the priceless inheritance of their countrymen to drink what they pleased, how-ever and wherever they pleased; dauntlessly they kept the skull-and-crossbones of self-indulgence flying from the modest turrets of every licensed victualler in Britain.

The fact that these bonny fighters all happened to be brewers did cause a little cynical comment from time to time, but just because a man occasionally finds himself in that most comfortable of all ethical positions, of asserting his morality and insuring his dividends at the same time, it does not necessarily follow that he is being insincere. A truth does not cease to be a truth just because a rich man believes it, and there certainly seemed to be no evidence in the private lives of the brewers that they were peddling commodities they weren't willing to consume themselves. Indeed, the virtuousness of the Wets was so rampant that it was not long before governments were besot-ted by it, and began elevating so many brewers to the Upper Chamber that it was not altogether unknown for the occasional ill-bred cynic to refer to the House of Lords as the Beerage.

Protesting Asquith's Licensing Bill in 1908

Speaker: "I ASK YOU—WHAT IS THE GREAT DRINK QUESTION?"
Voice: "WHAT ARE YOU GOING TO HAVE?"

DON'T LET YOUR HAT DROP OVER YOUR RED LIGHT,
MISTER, I DON'T WANT PINCHING!

entrenchment of the vested interests of the Wets. Even richer comedy followed four years later when Mr Asquith introduced his own licensing bill, which legislated that the number of public house licence-holders must be cut by one-third over the next fourteen years. Although the idea itself is funny, and although the implication that Mr Asquith believed anyone would still be taking him seriously in fourteen years' time is even funnier, the richest joke of all is that it should have been Mr Asquith of all people who expressed public concern over the quantity of alcohol being consumed by his fellow-countrymen. The Liberal leader could have effectively reduced that quantity simply by taking the oath himself; for him to offer a bill reducing alcoholic outlets was like M. Landru supporting a Married Women's Property Act. Even his friendliest biographers have assured us that Mr Asquith was often to be seen rising unsteadily from various tables of state after too intense a consultation with the brandy decanter. We laugh at him today not because he drank like a fish, but because he drank like a humbug.

When his absurd bill was introduced, cook and dog once again set upon the hand that had tried to feed them. The Temperance faction was mortified by the fourteen-year delay, while the Wets, expressing their reaction with customary moderation, described the bill as 'spoliation, brigandage, blackmail and hypocrisy'. A meeting held at the Cannon Street Hotel decided that Asquith had imperilled the savings of all working men who had invested in brewery shares, the white heat of indignation in the purlieus of Cannon Street being explained by the fact that everyone at the meeting was a brewery debenture holder. However, before we laugh too loudly at the antic disposition of Mr Asquith, we would do well to remember that in a sense he won the day after all. In 1915 he introduced a bill imposing an afternoon closure on all public houses, a temporary expedient to be dropped

However, the same statesmen who ennobled the beer salesmen were under constant pressure from the Drys to pour away the beer, an interesting dilemma which they resolved with a little empirical political philosophy, seeming to pour the beer away and then going home to fortify their troubled minds with a stiff snort. Even this policy had its dangers, for when you throw a bone to a mad dog, the cook will complain of the waste of a good bone even as the dog bites you because the bone has no meat on it, and it will not be long before cook and dog discover that the one thing they have in common is a passionate hatred of you. This is exactly what happened to poor Mr Gladstone in 1870, when he finally succumbed to the nagging of an organisation called the United Alliance for the Suppression of the Liquor Traffic and passed a bill bringing in heavier fines for drunkenness and shorter opening hours. The bill was condemned by the Alliance as feeble and by the publicans as oppressive, by which time Mr Gladstone must have been heartily sick of the whole business. Here he was being pelted by the liquor interests for having made the drinking of alcohol more difficult, and yet years before, when he had innocently legalised the sale of French wines in grocers' shops and its consumption in pastry-cook shops, the publicans had howled bloody murder over their concern for 'the traditional ways of the British constitution', by which presumably they meant that nobody should be allowed to hold a vested interest in drunkenness except them. In any event, the anxiety of the publicans proved to be unjustified; in 1875, five years after the passing of the bill, Britain recorded the most bibulous year in its history to date, when the annual per capita consumption of spirits was 1.3 gallons, and of beer an awe-inspiring 34.4 gallons.

The next piece of legislative pandering to the Temperance lobby followed in 1904, when a footling amendment by Mr Balfour to the licensing laws was so comically, and probably deliberately, ineffectual that measures supposedly calculated to placate the Drys were actually rejected by them as a further

SHAY, OLE MAN, YOU'RE ALL ON A COLD SWEAT.--TOO MUCH WHISKY, M'LAD!

SOME ARE PHOTOGRAPHED WITH THEIR WIVES, OTHERS WITH A FAVOURITE DOG---
BUT I CAN'T UNDERSTAND WHY SOME DON'T BE TAKEN LIKE THIS!

when the war was over. But Mr Asquith very cleverly omitted to say which war, with the result that the afternoon closure is with us to this very day.

What was all this buffoonery supposed to prove? Nobody apart from a few crackpots seriously believed the nation would ever embrace total abstinence, any more than it would ever countenance round-the-clock drinking. And yet the Wet-Dry quadrille continued. What campaigners on both sides failed to see is that drinking, like gambling and sex, is not one of those human activities which can be legislated away, and that restrictive acts of Parliament will not reduce drunkenness, but merely place the wherewithal to achieve it outside the law. When in 1903 J. A. Hobson reminded the country that it spent £180,000,000 a year on drink and less than half that amount on war, there must have been a great many people too foozled with beer to appreciate the ambivalent nature of those statistics.

Nobody stopped to think that perhaps the most effective way of reducing drunkenness was to offer people living conditions less calculated to hound them into the refuge of an alcoholic stupor. Cheap gin was known as 'the quickest way out of Manchester', and in the working-class districts of the great cities the local pub was usually the one haven of bright colour and convivial clamour. It is no coincidence that the problem of intemperance has become less urgent since Hogarth's day, as general conditions have become less unspeakable. But perhaps the Balfours and the Asquiths were more sapient than they seemed. Perhaps in conducting their daft games they were only playing for time to keep the ultimate folly off the statute book. That the British were right to prohibit Prohibition was proved with the tragic débâcle of the Volstead Act in the United States.

Meanwhile, what of the drinker down at the local? Unaware that his habit of bending his elbow had become a religious, a political, a psychological issue, he grew more and more befuddled as the years went by, not just from the beer but also from the law, which grew so confused that what was beyond it in one borough was well within it across the boundary lines in another. He continued to bend that elbow with stoic persistence, enduring always that special martyrdom of the drunkard, which is to suffer from one of the very few illnesses whose effects seem hilariously funny to the non-suffering onlooker. If some of the comic postcards which treat drink seem to contain predicaments too absurd even for slapstick humour, if we cannot accept the possibility of a man embracing a lamp-post and gazing up at its light under the impression it is a bedroom window, if we decide it is taking poetic licence too far to depict a drunk mounting the stairs of a bus and asking to be tucked

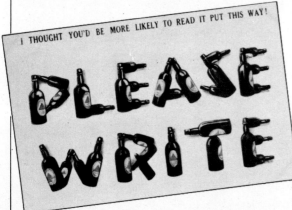

I THOUGHT YOU'D BE MORE LIKELY TO READ IT PUT THIS WAY!

PLEASE WRITE

in, if we continue to doubt whether in real life drunks still try to aim doorkeys at non-existent locks, then we might change our minds on all these counts when reading Bernard Shaw's affectionate reminiscence of his father:

A boy who has seen 'the governor' with an imperfectly wrapped-up goose under one arm and a ham in the same condition under the other (both purchased under heaven knows what delusion of festivity), butting at the garden wall in the belief that he was pushing open the gate, and transforming his tall hat to a concertina in the process, and who, instead of being overwhelmed with shame and anxiety at the spectacle, has been so disabled by merriment (uproariously shared by the maternal uncle) that he has hardly been able to rush to the rescue of the hat and pilot its wearer to safety, is clearly not a boy who will make tragedies of trifles instead of making trifles of tragedies. If you cannot get rid of the family skeleton, you may as well make it dance.

Nothing in this section is more outlandish than that glimpse of genteel life in Dublin a century ago, not even the extraordinary butchering of the English language incorporated in the immortal punning exchange:

'Is this Wembley?'
'No, it's Thursday.'
'So am I. Let's have a drink.'

The state of mind implied by that repartee has set new problems of technique both for the physician obliged to prescribe for it and the writer expected to describe it. It was that gallant philosopher Beachcomber who disclosed that the only effective cure for a red nose was to keep drinking till it turned purple, and that consummate lord of language P. G. Wodehouse who finally hit on a verbal arrangement to do

justice to the frantic choreography performed by a drunk staggering across the pavement after being forcibly ejected from a public house. Wodehouse defined it as 'like a man doing a foxtrot backwards'. Having spent the nights of the first thirty years of my life sleeping in a basement room whose window gave on to the legs of the customers of the local public house as they found their eccentric way home at eleven o'clock every night, I can vouch for the scientific accuracy of both Beachcomber's diagnosis and Wodehouse's definition. Perhaps the arrogance of my self-assertiveness on this point is explained away by W. C. Fields who, in an address impudently entitled 'The Temperance Lecture', observed that 'when a man takes a drink he thinks the world revolves around him; after three drinks it usually does.' But please do not dismiss my opinion too lightly; I'm not nearly as think as you drunk I am.

THERE'S A LOT O' TALK ABOUT "HAS BEENS," BUT LET ME TELL YOU, I'VE A FEW ARROWS IN MY QUIVER YET!

YOU SPEND THE NIGHT AT THE SWAN WITH TWO NECKS—SNAKES ACCOMPANY YOU HOME— THEN FOR THE DRAGON WITH TWO TONGUES!

AIN'T LIFE STRANGE?

NO,—BOOZED !

"THIS BEER'S A BIT THIN, LASS!"
"WHAT D'YOU EXPECT? THA'D BE
THIN IF THA'D BEEN PULLED
THROUGH T'SAME PIPE!"

GOOD HEAVENS! I DIDN'T KNOW
I WAS AS BALD AS THAT!

HI, MISTER, YER
LOSING YER YO-YO!

CHEERIO! HERE'S LOOKING AT YOU
ALL THE WAY

"DAMN IT ALF—THAT BLASTED TRAIN'S FRIGHTENED ALL THE FISH AWAY!"

"I MISS THAT **SPITTOON** YOU HAD HERE."
"YOU **ALWAYS DID**, THAT'S WHY IT'S GONE!"

"I'VE GOT A BOTTLE OF WHISKY FOR THE WIFE!"
"THA'SH A **VERY GOOD SWAP**, OLD MAN!"

HANG ON, MISSUS! I'LL HAVE YOU OUT IN A COUPLE O' MINISH!

"WHAT ARE YOU DOING, MAC?"
"GOT A FLY IN MA BEER, AN' AH'M WRINGING IT OOT!"

"HADN'T A CHANCE OFFICER—**SHE RAN STRAIGHT ACROSS THE ROAD!**"

"IS THIS WEMBLEY?"
"NO IT'S THURSDAY!"
"SO AM I—LET'S HAVE A DRINK!"

12
THE END OF THE LINE

In Dundee halfway up a hill climbing from the Canongate to Dens Park, there used to be a theatrical boarding house whose draughty rooms, with their elaborate cornices and massive mantelpieces, were filled with giggling chorus girls from the local variety theatre, one or two medical students, and a few bewildered musicians from the town's three rococo dance halls. It was, you might say, a flighty sort of establishment; the mistress had never quite managed to marry herself to the master, and the traffic between rooms would never really have commended itself to the Festival of Light. And yet even in that free-for-all of an establishment, where the last call for supper was in the middle of the night and bed-and-breakfast often meant sleeping in the bath, there were certain things that were 'not done', certain defiant gestures by the proprietress which indicated that she still clung, with a kind of nostalgic respect for her own very distant girlhood, to the remnants of respectability. I can state with the authority of a one-time resident that she would not have approved of the contents of this book – or rather, she would have pretended not to.

In the hall of that vanished house there hung on the wall one of those baize letter-racks in which the morning's mail was slipped, so that each of us, as we staggered out of the front door to meet a new day, could take what had been sent to us. None of the chorus girls were intellectual giants, giantesque though they may have been in certain other respects, and they appeared to maintain contact with the outside world only through the use of the kind of postcards which Messrs Bamforth so obligingly manufactured. There was never a morning when there were not at least three or four of the cards waiting in that green baize rack, and it seemed extraordinary to me that every time I passed them they were always facing with the handwriting upwards, so that the illustrations were concealed. Admittedly this was the only practical arrangement, because with the handwriting uppermost it became easy to see for whom the card was intended. But that was not a household distinguished for its practical arrangements. The explanation came to me when I arose unusually early at the crack of noon one day and came downstairs looking for letters, to find our landlady, in an uneasy compromise between lingerie and total nudity, turning all the cards round in the letter-holder so that the drawings and captions were hidden. She was saying in effect that though she might countenance a bit of slap-and-tickle, and even indulge in it herself, she was running a decent establishment; you had to draw the line somewhere, and that somewhere was the postcards.

That was in 1950 and I wonder whether that gallantly moralistic proprietress would have gone to the same lengths today to keep hers an orderly house. In the years since I lived under her roof, the British have been unbuttoning at a most indecorous rate, and concentrating on the pleasurable task of gaining belated revenge on the Victorians for having sold the nation that package of lies and deceit and madness which went under the name of sexual morality. Which means that what was scandalous only the day before yesterday might seem tameness incarnate today. Why conceal postcard illustrations when the daily life out in the streets is acknowledging every moment the truisms which the cards represent? Is it possible that the British can liberate themselves to a point where candid vulgarity is no longer interesting? Cyril Kersh has written a novel called *The Diabolical Liberties of Uncle Max* in which the hero, a back-street pornographer, is ruined by the sudden flood of his wares in the respectable bookshops. Are the saucy postcards doomed to the same fate?

Probably not. The cards commend themselves to successive generations, not just because they are vulgar but also because they are very often funny. They raise a laugh about one of the most ridiculous aspects of humanity, its dreams of copulation, and because they raise a laugh they claim an existence which is independent of the morality which gave birth to them. The cards are disrespectful, ignoble, lecherous, crude, coarse, vulgar, disgraceful. They are all these things, but they are also funny, and that is their salvation. They appeal, and will continue to appeal, to the worst side of our nature, which, being the dominant side, usually gets what it wants in the end. They will continue to be popular because they amuse us, and remind us of what we used to find comical. As Orwell once said of them, they represent the worm's-eye view. And in a world so densely populated with worms, that surely spells survival.

THE END

Photographs and illustrations were supplied by, or are reproduced by kind permission of the following:
British Leyland, Family Planning Association (photographs Gus Coral), Mander and Mitchenson Theatre Collection, Mansell Collection, Popperfoto, H.M. Postmaster-General, Radio Times Hulton Picture Library, Barnaby's Picture Library, Sotheby's Belgravia, and Iain Gaynor.
Photography research by Philippa Lewis.

The author and publishers wish to thank the following for permission to reproduce copyright material in this volume. Edward Arnold Ltd: *Howard's End* E. M. Forster; B. T. Batsford Ltd: *Victorian England* W. J. Reader; Geoffrey Bles Ltd: *Nocturne* Frank Swinnerton; The Bodley Head Ltd: *Collected Letters* G. Bernard Shaw, *My Autobiography* Charles Chaplin; Cassell & Co., Ltd: *Full Score* Neville Cardus, *Goodbye to All That* Robert Graves; William Collins Sons & Co., Ltd: *Autobiography* Neville Cardus, *English Saga, 1840-1940*, Sir Arthur Bryant; Constable & Co., Ltd: Preface to *Immaturity* G. Bernard Shaw; David and Charles Ltd: *Edwardian Life and Leisure* Ronald Pearsall; J. M. Dent & Sons Ltd: *Book of London Yesterdays* Frederick Willis; Hamish Hamilton Ltd: *The First World War* A. J. P. Taylor; Hart-Davis MacGibbon Ltd: *The Strange Death of Liberal England* George Dangerfield; William Heinemann Ltd: *The Edwardians* J. B. Priestley; Oxford University Press: *Autobiography* Anthony Trollope, *The Great War in Modern Memory* Paul Fussell, *Oxford History of England* Sir Robert Ensor; Secker and Warburg Ltd: *My Country Right or Left 1940-43* George Orwell, *You Can't Be Too Careful* H. G. Wells; Weidenfeld & Nicolson Ltd: *Victoria RI* Elizabeth Longford.

Every effort has been made to trace the copyright holders of photographs and quoted material. Should there be any omissions in this respect, we apologise and shall be pleased to make the appropriate acknowledgement in future editions.